Short Cuts

Dedication

To my wife, the finest teacher I know, who tested chapters in her classroom, gave suggestions, even helped proofread despite her busy schedule—but most of all, gave me encouragement when it was most needed.

Short Cuts

BOOK 2

An Interactive English Course

James Mentel

Los Angeles Unified School District

McGraw-Hill

Boston, Massachusetts   Burr Ridge, Illinois   Dubuque, Iowa
Madison, Wisconsin   New York, New York   San Francisco, California   St. Louis, Missouri

McGraw-Hill

A Division of The **McGraw·Hill** *Companies*

Short Cuts
An Interactive English Course
Book Two

2 3 4 5 6 7 8 9 0 VNH   VNH 9 0 3 2 1 0 9 8 7

ISBN 0-07-041887-X

This book was set in Caslon Regular by York Graphic Services, Inc. The editor was Tim Stookesberry; the interior designer was Niza Hanany, the front and back matter designer was Suzanne Montazer; the production supervisor was Tanya Nigh; the cover was designed by Francis Owens; the cover and interior illustrator was Dave Sullivan; interior icons were designed by Marcus Badgley and Pam Webster.

Photographic credits: page 103, *top,* © David Woo, Stock Boston; page 103, *bottom,* © Sheryl Maeder; page 111, © Spencer Grant, Stock Boston.

Von Hoffman Press, Jefferson City, MO, was printer and binder.
Phoenix Color Corporation was cover separator and printer.

Library of Congress Catalog Card Number: 96-77577

INTERNATIONAL EDITION
Copyright 1996. Exclusive rights by The McGraw-Hill Companies, Inc. for manufacture and export. This book cannot be re-exported from the country to which it is consigned by McGraw-Hill. The International Edition is not available in North America.

When ordering this title, use ISBN 0-07-114519-2

Contents

STRUCTURE GOALS	COMPETENCIES	RECOGNITION

CHAPTER 1 / A Living Room   1

Students will have a sense of the form of . . .	Students will be able to . . .	Students may understand and use some examples of . . .
• **there is/there are** (the non-referential **there**) in the present and past tenses • prepositions of place	• ask for and give directions for placing objects • ask for and give a basic description of the place they live • introduce someone	• past form of non-referential **there** (**there was/there were**) • past tense of some common irregular verbs (**sat, read**)

CHAPTER 2 / Getting Around   13

Students will have a sense of the form of . . .	Students will be able to . . .	Students may understand and use some examples of . . .
• imperatives • polite requests with **would, could,** and **can**	• ask and give directions to a location • ask about and give a general description of a neighborhood • ask for clarification	• comparatives (**lower, better**)

CHAPTER 3 / Likes and Dislikes   25

Students will have a sense of the form of . . .	Students will be able to . . .	Students may understand and use some examples of . . .
• present tense statements and questions • verb plus infinitive • frequency adverbs	• ask and answer questions about free-time activities • discuss the relative frequency of various activities • show interest during conversations	• **and** and **but** to connect independent clauses

STRUCTURE GOALS	COMPETENCIES	RECOGNITION

STRUCTURE GOALS	COMPETENCIES	RECOGNITION

CHAPTER 8 / The Calendar — 85

Students will have a sense of the form of . . .
- the future with **be going to**
- past tense, especially question formation
- ordinal numbers

Students will be able to . . .
- accept or refuse an offer for an appointment
- discuss future plans in friendly conversation
- discuss past events in friendly conversation
- excuse themselves following accidents

Students may understand and use some examples of . . .
- polite invitations
- **had better** (periphrastic modal indicating necessity)

CHAPTER 9 / Classic Movies — 97

Students will have a sense of the form of . . .
- object pronouns
- the differences between the use of the simple present, present continuous, and past tenses

Students will be able to . . .
- express likes and dislikes about movies, along a continuum
- agree with someone (using **I do, too; So do I;** or **Me, too**)
- ask and answer questions about the time of an event

Students may understand and use some examples of . . .
- the simple present tense to describe books or movies

CHAPTER 10 / A Dream House — 109

Students will have a sense of the form of . . .
- quantifiers (**much, many, a little, a few**)
- questions with **how much** or **how many** (count/noncount distinction)

Students will be able to . . .
- describe a house or apartment using **it has**
- describe a place using **there is/there are** and quantifiers
- use **I'd like** to express a preference

Students may understand and use some examples of . . .
- similes

From the Author

Dear Colleagues,

I developed these materials by trying out ideas in real adult English classrooms over many years. I was influenced by theories and research about language acquisition, but in the end, what influenced me most was what worked. The things that worked are here in the book—the things that didn't work, are not. Most of all, my goal was to provide teachers with tools that would allow their natural creativity to bloom. I've been continually amazed at the creativity of ESOL teachers, and all too often materials have confined that creativity rather than encouraged it.

These are materials, not a method. My hope is that they are like a very solid, well-made tool that a carpenter can use day after day in many different ways and situations, creating many different projects. Although the **Teacher's Manual** provides exact, step-by-step directions about one way to use the materials, I've been happy to find that almost all teachers who have used the materials have come up with their own creative ways to use them, ways that fit their own teaching style and student population.

As teachers, we are all explorers and researchers. The more we explore and invent, the more exciting language teaching becomes, and the more exciting language learning becomes. I hope you will share some of your results with me by writing me in care of my publisher.

I feel extremely fortunate to be publishing these materials with McGraw-Hill, and I'd like to thank a number of people there for their intelligence, bravery, and good humor throughout the entire process. I would especially like to thank my editor, Tim Stookesberry, who "got it" right from the beginning. I would also like to acknowledge the rest of the editorial and production team who worked so painstakingly on these materials: Eve Strock, Tanya Nigh, Francis Owens, Michelle Lyon, Cheryl Pavlik, Stephanie Weiss, Bill Preston, Gina Martinez, Pam Tiberia, Brett Glass, and the wonderfully talented artist, Dave Sullivan. Finally, I'd like to thank Thalia Dorwick, Mike DePasquale, Carole O'Keefe, Jerry Hagan, Tom Allumbaugh, Roxan Kinsey, Margaret Metz, Ann Cunningham, and the rest of the McGraw-Hill sales and marketing department for their outstanding support.

Sincerely,

To the Teacher

Short Cuts is a three-level series for teaching English to young adult and adult students. Each level of the program contains the following components:

1. a student text
2. a teacher's manipulative kit (available in two versions)
3. an optional teacher's audio tape
4. an optional student audio tape
5. a teacher's manual

Using Manipulatives

A unique feature of *Short Cuts* is its use of manipulatives, or cut-ups. The use of these manipulatives:

- addresses a variety of learning styles: visual, aural, and kinesthetic;
- provides immediate feedback for both teacher and student;
- focuses students' attention on accomplishing specific tasks during an extended receptive period;
- encourages the use of English for the negotiation of meaning through student interaction;
- provides opportunities for student-centered cooperative learning.

Perhaps the best reasons for using manipulatives are that they are fun, they create student interest, and they work! Using them is a little like playing a computer game, and it's a lot more fun to do that than to sit passively and listen to the teacher. The manipulatives in the *Short Cuts* program have been used with grandmothers and gang-members, and the reaction has always been positive.

The teacher is also provided with his/her own manipulatives that can be used to model language and for other communicative classroom activities. The teacher's version of both the worksheet and manipulatives is found in the *Teacher's Manipulative Kit* (see description on page xvi).

Each of the ten chapters in the student text is organized around a theme. The accompanying student worksheets and manipulatives used to complete many of the exercises and activities in the chapters correspond to these themes. The student worksheets and manipulatives are located in perforated pages in the back of the student text. The smaller pictures along the side and bottom of the worksheets are the manipulatives—they should be cut or torn out. The *Teacher's Manual* contains many more helpful suggestions for ways to use these materials in the classroom.

Recommended Proficiency Levels

Book Two of the *Short Cuts* program is designed for low-beginning to high-beginning students who are not true beginners. Typically, students at this level have some limited ability to read and write in English. They may understand simple conversations in English when they hear them but probably have difficulty producing spoken language. *Book Two* has been written to conform to the ESL Beginning-High level of the California Model Standards.

Short Cuts is also compatible with the Comprehensive Adult Student Assessment System (CASAS) and the Student Performance Levels (SPLs) recommended by the Mainstream English Language Training (MELT) project of the U.S. Department of Health and Human Services. SPL scores shown below are correlated with scores on the Basic English Skills Test (BEST).

Grammar coverage can also be used to determine placement. *Short Cuts, Book Two* contains the following grammar topics: *there is / there are*, imperatives, simple present, simple past, verb plus infinitive, the modal *can*, simple present versus present continuous, future with *will*, and future with *be going to*.

	MELT SPLs	BEST Scores	CASAS Achievements Scores
Short Cuts Book One	0 and I	0–15	165–190
Short Cuts Book Two	II	16–28	181–190
Short Cuts Book Three	III	29–41	191–208

A Visual Tour of This Text

This visual tour is designed to acquaint you with the key features of the student textbook, as well as to give you suggestions of at least one way to teach those features.

The essential teaching elements for the **Short Cuts** program are self-contained in the student text. This book provides between 100–130 hours of instruction in all four language skills—listening, speaking, reading, and writing—as well as additional instruction in the essential grammar structures typically introduced at this level.

The Opening Page

Each chapter revolves around a central theme or content focus. The opening page is a visual depiction of this theme and includes most of the key chapter vocabulary. It also serves as a reference for students as they work through each section of the chapter. In addition, students refer back to this page to check their answers in the self-review **On Your Own** section at the end of the chapter.

CHAPTER 5

Weather in the World

Moscow — snowing
20° cold

Paris partly cloudy
45° cool

Mexico City — raining
70° warm

New York
humid
smoggy
90° hot

Hong Kong
cloudy 65° warm
foggy

Lagos
sunny
windy
85° hot

Focus On
- contrast simple present and present continuous tenses
- frequency adverbs
  - *always*
  - *usually*
  - *often*
- describing the weather
- weather vocabulary
- how to discuss the weather

49

Focus On

The **Focus On** box gives both teachers and students a quick glance at the most important elements of the chapter.

The Worksheet

Located in perforated pages in the back of the student text, the worksheet contains a simplified version of the picture found in the chapter opener, as well as the student manipulatives. This page should be torn out every time the class is ready to start a new chapter in **Short Cuts**, as it will be the focus for many of the activities in each lesson.

Manipulatives

The manipulatives, or cut-outs, are the pictures found at the edges of the worksheet. Students will either tear or cut them out with scissors and move them around on their worksheets to complete many of the listening, speaking, reading, and writing activities found in the chapter.

Tips on Using the Worksheet

The **Teacher's Manual** includes a number of suggestions on how to use the worksheet and manipulatives. It's a good idea to encourage your students to collect and store their manipulatives with either a paperclip or an envelope at the end of each lesson. You should also keep a few extra photocopies of the worksheet page on hand for emergencies!

Each chapter contains four two-page sections (called **Situations**) that practice all four skills and are meant to be self-contained lessons lasting 2–3 hours.

A Visual Introduction

The teacher begins the lesson by presenting a chunk of language using materials from the *Teacher's Kit* and the visual dialogue found in the **Situation**. In this sample, the chunk includes phrases such as *What's the temperature?*, *It's (a temperature in degrees)*, *That's (hot, warm, cool, or cold)*.

Examples

The examples are visual references for any extra information students may need to do the listening and group work.

Listening Exercises

After the target language has been adequately modeled, students arrange their worksheet pictures in response to a listening activity conducted by the teacher. The teacher has many options here—she/he can use the *Teacher's Tape* that is provided for these sections or the tapescript in the back of the student text to conduct this period of active listening. This section gives students the opportunity to be actively involved in a fun and challenging activity without having to produce language. By looking at the students' worksheets, the teacher gets immediate feedback on how much each student understands.

•GROUP WORK•

Students form groups and practice on their own. In most instances, they will be using their worksheet in response to various tasks and activities associated with the lesson's main teaching focus. Since they are using language to do specific tasks, students are forced to listen carefully and negotiate meaning. Often this requires the use of clarification devices. (*I'm sorry . . . Did you say warm or hot?*). Because such interactive activities are fun, students will practice longer and with more sustained interest.

Reading

Read this, and put your pictures in the correct places on your worksheet.

TRAVELER'S WEATHER REPORT

If you're traveling to Mexico City, don't forget your suntan lotion. It's sunny and hot there today. They're expecting temperatures in the high nineties.

If you're going to New York, take your umbrella. It's raining right now, and the temperature is in the low fifties.

If you're heading for Hong Kong, hold on to your hat. It's very windy—gusts up to 20 miles per hour. The temperature is mild—72 degrees.

Writing

Complete these sentences. Then share your answers with the class.

1. It's cold. Don't forget your _____.
2. It's 99 degrees. Bring your _____.
3. It's cool. Don't forget your _____.
4. It's raining. Bring your _____.
5. It's snowing. Bring your _____.
6. It's foggy. Don't forget your _____.

 Extra *Write weather reports for three cities. Use sentences like those above. Then read your reports to the class. They will put their pictures in the correct places on their worksheets.*

SITUATION *C* **55**

Extra

Sprinkled throughout all chapters, the **Extra** boxes provide students with an additional twist on a given chapter activity. In this example, students write imaginary weather reports for various cities that appear on their worksheets. They are then encouraged to read their writing passages aloud to their group or the whole class, who will use the information to complete a listening activity.

Reading

There are two types of readings in this book. The first type, as shown in this example, recycles the structures and vocabulary of the lesson, while adding new ones. Students can work in groups or individually and arrange their worksheets to reflect their understanding of the reading. The teacher can check comprehension by looking at the students' worksheets. The second type of reading in *Short Cuts, Book Two* often features either authentic or adapted source materials. Here, students are provided with either a vocabulary labeling activity or some other short written task to facilitate reading comprehension.

Writing

In each chapter, the writing activities contain a range of controlled to more open-ended tasks. In this particular example, students need only supply additional vocabulary items; but even something as simple as this—when shared with the class—can become a rich source of language input for all. In many of the book's writing activities, students arrange their manipulatives on their worksheet as a kind of "brainstorming" activity. Then, by circulating throughout the classroom, the teacher will be able to see what the student is trying to write about and be able to offer the kind of help that is needed. Most of the writing activities in *Short Cuts* offer enough flexibility to allow students a lot of room for personal communication in their writing—there are rarely "right or wrong" answers.

This two-page spread introduces the important structural elements of the chapter. Grammar is first introduced pictorially. In this example, students will learn the difference between the simple present and present continuous tenses when talking about the weather. The grammar symbols that are used in these pictorial explanations are consistent throughout the entire three-level *Short Cuts* program. *Note:* Although the **Grammar Check** section appears at the end of each chapter, teachers may introduce it at any point in the lesson (at their own discretion).

A. Simple present tense vs. present continuous tense

We use the **simple present tense** when we talk about something that is generally true, that happens all the time, or that happens from time to time.

April   May   June   July

It rains a lot.

We use the **present continuous tense** when we talk about something that is happening now.

It's raining right now.

B. Simple present tense

We use the base form of verbs in the simple present tense. We add **s** or **es** for **he, she,** and **it**.

V s

rains   a lot.

...s plus the negative word **not**.

aux s V

doesn't   rain   a lot.

World

C. Present continuous tense

To form the present continuous tense, we use **be** plus the simple form of the verb plus **-ing**.

 Be   V ing

It   is   raining.

The negative form looks like this.

 Be   V ing

It   isn't   raining.

SIMPLE PRESENT TENSE			
I You We They	(don't)	work	every day. on Saturdays. at home. a lot.
He She	(doesn't)	work	

PRESENT CONTINUOUS TENSE				
I	am			
You We They	are	(not)	working	now.
He She	is			

•EXERCISE•

Complete the sentences with the simple present or present continuous tense. Use the charts above for reference.

1. We _____ to the park every afternoon.
   go

2. It _____ in New York in July.
   (negative) + snow

3. They _____ right now.
   sleep

4. I _____ on Sundays.
   (negative) + work

5. She _____ English now.
   study

GRAMMAR BOXES

The right-hand page includes more traditional grammar boxes that students can use as a reference to complete the exercise that follows.

•EXERCISES•

The grammar exercises are completely tied to the context of the chapter's theme. They often refer in some way to the picture on the opening page.

Reading

Read this, and put your pictures in the correct places on your worksheet.

MY LIVING ROOM

My living room is very nice. There are three windows. There are two windows on the right side, and there is one window on the far wall. There's a sofa on the right side. There's an armchair against the far wall. There's an end table next to the armchair, on the right, and there's a lamp on the table. There's a bookcase on the left side of the room. There's a TV on the bookcase. In the middle of the room, there's a rug. There isn't a telephone in my living room.

Writing

Write about your living room (or an imaginary living room).

_____

_____

_____

_____

_____

_____

_____

 *Read your story to the class. They will put their pictures in the correct places on their worksheets.*

Bobby and his grandfather are talking about the past.

When I was a small boy, our living room was very small. But it was bright and sunny.

There were two windows, on the right. And there was a big armchair on the right, under the window.

There was one window.

There were two windows.

There were no windows.

 Listen

Listen and put your pictures in the correct places on your worksheet.

GROUP WORK

Describe a living room. Put your pictures on your worksheet. Then clear your worksheets. Take turns asking questions like these to put your pictures together again. Use **was** and **were.**

There were two windows.

One window was on the left.

And there was a sofa on the left.

Reading/Writing

Read this, and put your pictures in the correct places on your worksheet.

AN IMPORTANT MEMORY

When I was a little boy, the house we lived in was very small. There was only one window in the living room, but it was a big window, and the living room was usually very sunny.

There was a sofa on the right side of the living room, under the window. It was an old sofa, full of rips and holes. But it was very comfortable. There was a worn Oriental rug in front of it.

I remember sitting on the sofa with my mother. There was an end table with a chipped lamp on it, next to the sofa on the left. At night, my mother and I sat on the sofa next to the lamp and read books. When I was very little, my mother read to me. Then, when I was older, I read my own books, and my mother read her books.

This is a memory I think about a lot.

What words can you label from the story?

_____

_____

rips

_____

Now complete these sentences to describe the picture.

1. There was a ___big_____ window.

2. There _____ an old ___sofa_____.

3. _____ _____ a chipped _____ on the table.

4. There _____ a worn _____ in front of the sofa.

There is/there are

When we describe places we often use **there is** or **there are**.

| There | is | a sofa | in | my living room. |

When we speak, we usually make a contraction.

| There's | a sofa | in | my living room. |

Two or more things use **are.**

| There | are | two windows | in | my living room. |

Questions look like this: (Move **be** to the left of **there.**)

| Is | there | a telephone | in | your living room? |

In the past tense, we change **is** to **was** and **are** to **were.**

| There | was | a sofa | in | my living room. |

| There | were | two windows | in | my living room. |

THERE IS/THERE ARE

PRESENT TENSE

There	is 's	an armchair a sofa one window	in the room.
	are	two windows three windows	

PAST TENSE

There	was	an armchair a sofa one window	in the room.
	were	two windows three windows	

QUESTIONS AND ANSWERS

Is there	an armchair a sofa a bookcase	in your living room?
Are there	windows a lot of windows	

There isn't	a sofa. a rug.
There's no	sofa. rug.

•EXERCISE•

Look at the picture on page 1. Fill in the blanks in this story about the picture.

1. _____ There _____ _____ are _____ two people in the living room.

2. _____ _____ a purple sofa against the far wall.

3. _____ _____ a lot of books in the _____.

4. _____ _____ a telephone on the _____ side of the room.

5. _____ _____ a rug in the _____ of the room.

6. _____ _____ two boots in the _____.

7. _____ _____ curtains on the _____.

8. _____.

9. _____.

Vocabulary

Do you know these words? Find them on page 1.

- ❏ window
- ❏ lamp
- ❏ sofa
- ❏ large table

- ❏ rug
- ❏ floor
- ❏ bookcase
- ❏ armchair

- ❏ telephone
- ❏ picture
- ❏ end table
- ❏ closet

- ❏ the left side
- ❏ the far wall
- ❏ the right side
- ❏ the middle of the room

Listening

Listen to your tape, and put your pictures in the correct places on your worksheet. Then check your answer on page 1.

Nancy: I like my apartment a lot. It's sunny because there are two windows—one is on the far wall and the other window is on the left side of the room. There's a big purple sofa against the far wall, under the window. Next to the sofa, on the right, there's a bookcase. I read a lot, and there are a lot of books in the bookcase. On the bookcase, there's a lamp.

There's a large wooden table on the left side of the room, under the window, and my TV is on the table. There's a red armchair on the right side of the room. It's very comfortable. Next to the armchair on the left there's a small end table. My telephone is on the end table.

How to
introduce someone

Extra *Introduce two of your classmates.*

Getting Around

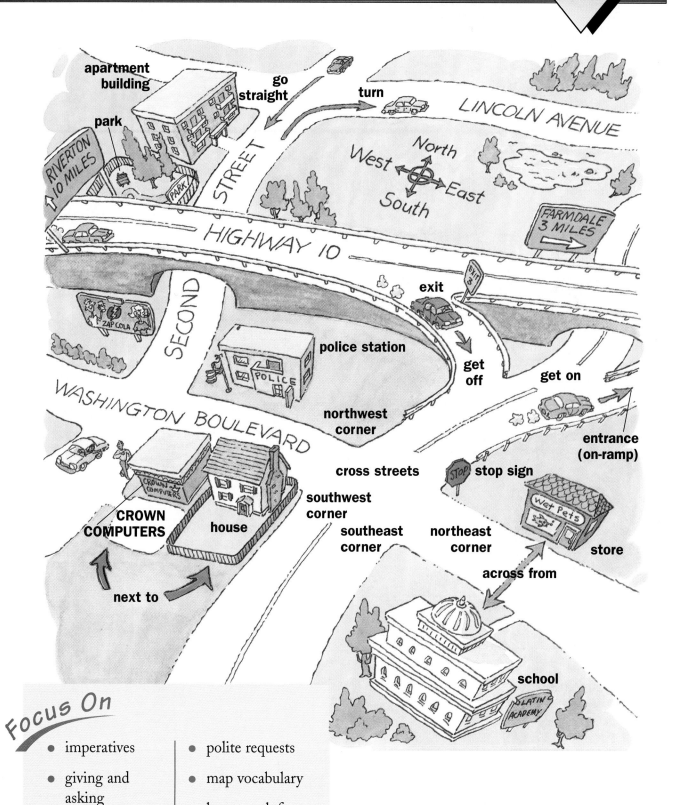

apartment building · go straight · turn · LINCOLN AVENUE · park · RIVERTON 10 MILES · North · West · East · South · FARMDALE 3 MILES · STREET · HIGHWAY 10 · exit · SECOND · ZAP COLA · police station · get off · get on · POLICE · northwest corner · entrance (on-ramp) · WASHINGTON BOULEVARD · cross streets · stop sign · STOP · Wet Pets · CROWN COMPUTERS · house · southwest corner · store · southeast corner · northeast corner · across from · next to · school · LATIN ACADEMY

Focus On

- imperatives
- giving and asking directions
- polite requests
- map vocabulary
- how to ask for clarification

Crown Computers is busy today.

Good afternoon, Crown Computers.

What time do you close?

Six o'clock.

OK. And where are you located?

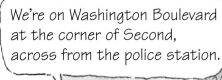

We're on Washington Boulevard at the corner of Second, across from the police station.

Thanks a lot.

Listen

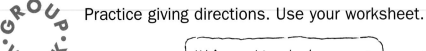

Listen and put your pictures in the correct places on your worksheet.

GROUP·WORK·

Practice giving directions. Use your worksheet.

Where are you located?

We're on Lincoln Avenue at the corner of First, across from the supermarket.

Reading

Read this, and put your pictures in the correct places on your worksheet.

CROWN COMPUTERS

Before you buy a computer, check out
CROWN COMPUTERS.

**We have the <u>lowest</u> prices in town. Nobody sells computers at better prices.
Crown Computers is located on Third Street, just south of Lincoln Avenue.
We're right across the street from exit 3 off Highway 10, conveniently next to
the highway entrance.**

Come see us soon!

Writing

Imagine you have a store. Write about your store. What kind of store is it?
Where is it?

Before you buy _____, check out

_____. We have the lowest prices in town.

Nobody sells _____ at better prices.

We're located _____

_____

_____.

Come see us soon!

 *Read your ad to the class. They will put their pictures in the
correct places on their worksheets.*

Al and Josie are talking about their free time.

Do you like to go to the movies, Al?

I love to. How about you?

Yeah. Quite a bit.

Maybe we could go together one of these days.

Do you like to  **?**

No, not at all.		A little.		Some.		Yes, I really like to.

| No. I hate to. | | No, not very much. | | Kind of. | | Yes, quite a bit. | I love to. |

Listen

Listen and put your pictures in the correct places on your worksheet.

GROUP WORK

Practice asking and answering questions like these. Use your worksheet.

Do you like to go to the movies, Antonio?

Kind of. How about you, Magda?

Not very much.

Readi

Read this,

Reading

Read this, and put your pictures in the correct places on your worksheet.

> I don't have much free time because I work, and I go to school, too. When I have free time, I love to go to the movies. I also like to watch TV quite a bit. One thing I don't do in my free time is cook. I hate to cook!

> I don't have much free time either. When I have free time, I love to play sports. I really like to read, too. My sister always wants to go shopping. I don't like to go shopping very much.

Writ

Write abo

1. I _____

2. I _____

3. I som

4. I _____

5. I harc

6. I nev

7. _____

8. _____

9. _____

10. _____

11. _____

Extr

Writing

Write about your likes and dislikes.

1. I love to _____.

2. I like to _____ quite a bit.

3. I like to _____ a little.

4. I don't like to _____ very much.

5. I don't like to _____ at all.

6. _____.

7. _____.

8. _____.

9. _____.

10. _____.

Mary Ann is in the electronics section of a department store. She's looking for a new TV.

How much is the twenty-five-inch TV?

Four hundred and forty-nine dollars.

That's kind of expensive.

Yes, but it's a very good TV.

$449

More formal	four hundred and forty-nine dollars four hundred and forty-nine
Less formal	four forty-nine four hundred and forty-nine bucks

Listen

Listen and put your pictures in the correct places on your worksheet.

GROUP WORK

Practice asking about prices. Use your worksheet.

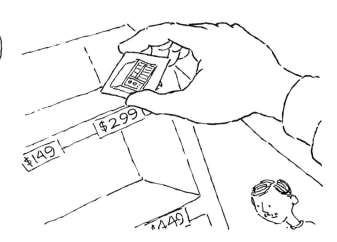

How much is the air conditioner?

Two hundred and ninety-nine dollars.

Left margin (partially visible):

Diana... free...

Do you... to the...

Really? two kid...

Never.

List...

GROU

WOR

Reading

Read this, and put your pictures in the correct places on your worksheet.

KENNY'S SHOPPING TRIP

Kenny is shopping for a present for his wife's birthday. She wants a new TV. The store has a 25-inch TV, but it costs $449. That's too much money for Kenny. He only has $150. Kenny asks the salesman for help. He says that the electronics store also has a 19-inch TV, and it's on sale for $149. Kenny can afford that. The salesman says it's a good deal, so Kenny is thinking about buying it.

Writing

What do you want for your birthday?

1. I want _____.

Ask other students what they want for their birthdays.

2. _____ wants _____.

3. _____ wants _____.

4. _____ wants _____.

5. _____ wants _____.

6. _____ wants _____.

7. _____ wants _____.

John is looking for a TV. Frank is with him.

How much is the nineteen-inch TV?

A hundred and forty-nine dollars.

Frank, could I borrow fifty dollars?

OK.

I'll take it.

OK. That's one hundred forty-nine dollars.

LEND   **BORROW**

Frank

John

Frank is lending John $50.

John is borrowing $50 from Frank.

Listen

Listen and put your pictures in the correct places on your worksheet.

GROUP WORK

Use your worksheet and give prices to all the items. Then role-play buying things. You can borrow money.

How much is the air conditioner?

Two hundred and forty-nine dollars.

Antonio, could I borrow one hundred and fifty dollars?

OK.

Reading/Writing

Read this, and complete the lines below.

A PROBLEM WITH A FRIEND

Last week, John borrowed $50 from Frank. He said, "Frank, I'll pay you back on Monday."

On Monday, Frank saw John at work. "Hey, John," he said. "Do you have my $50?"

"Oh, not today, Frank," said John. "I'll pay you back tomorrow."

On Tuesday, Frank saw John again. "Hi, John. Do you have my $50 today?"

"Oh, uh . . . no, but I'll pay you back on Thursday, for sure," said John.

On Thursday, Frank saw John at work. "John, I need my $50."

"Oh yeah," said John. "Tomorrow. I'll pay you back tomorrow. I promise."

Now, Frank is getting a little angry. He's thinking that it was a mistake to lend money to a friend.

What did they say?

Do you have my $50?

Monday

Tuesday

Thursday

Extra   *Work in groups. Continue the story.*

Frank is shopping.

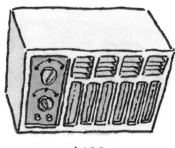

$99   **$149**   **$199**   **$249**

HERE'S A PROBLEM

Frank can buy the microwave.

He can buy the 19-inch TV.

He can't buy the air conditioner.

How much money does Frank have?
❏ $100   ❏ $150   ❏ $200

How much money does Frank have? Listen and point to the correct amount in the box above.

GROUP WORK Play a game. Use the prices above. Then talk about what Frank can buy and what he can't buy. The others guess. How much money does Frank have?

He can buy the microwave.
He can't buy the nineteen-inch TV.

He has one hundred and fifty dollars.

Sorry, that's wrong.

Right.

He has one hundred dollars.

Reading

Read these ads, and put your pictures in the correct places on your worksheet.

Sadai VCR
299.⁹⁹

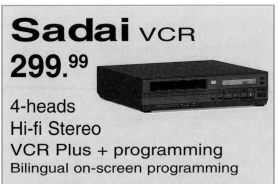

4-heads
Hi-fi Stereo
VCR Plus + programming
Bilingual on-screen programming

SADAI
25" Color TV
249.99

after $20
mail-in rebate

Stereo Sound   On-screen display
Auto programming   181 channels

Jang CD player
199.⁹⁹

only $10 a month
Remote stereo shelf system
6-disc CD changer
AM/FM tuner
Dual cassette deck

$899.⁹⁹ Jang
8 mm camcorder

with many features

optical 12:1 power zoom lens
auto focus system

$1099.⁹⁹
PACIFIC COMPUTER

Pentium processor
1.5 MB hard drive
24 MB RAM
CD ROM
Modem

Writing

Mary Ann is shopping. Use the prices above. Write a problem. First, how much money does she have? Then write about what she can buy and what she can't buy.

Mary Ann has $ _____.

1. She can buy _____.

2. She can't buy _____.

3. _____.

4. _____.

5. _____.

6. _____.

Read your sentences to the class. They will try to guess how much money Mary Ann has.

Cindy is looking for a new stereo system.

It's very well made.
It's a good buy.
It has a lot of features.
It's our best one.

Listen

Listen and put your pictures in the correct places on your worksheet.

GROUP WORK

Role-play that one student is the customer and one student is the salesperson. Use your worksheet. Practice borrowing money, too.

Reading

Read this, and underline the words from the ad on page 43.

A GOOD SALESMAN

Cindy went shopping yesterday. She was looking for a new stereo system. The salesman showed Cindy a very nice system. It cost $199.99.

"That's kind of expensive," said Cindy.

"But it's an excellent system," said the salesman.

"I don't know," said Cindy. "Maybe I should think about it."

"This stereo has a 6-disc CD changer," said the salesman.

"Hmmm . . . that's nice, but I don't have many CDs," said Cindy. "I have a lot of cassettes, though."

"Did I tell you that it also has a dual cassette deck?" said the salesman.

"I just don't know if I should buy it today," said Cindy.

"Well, it's on sale. This system usually costs $300," said the salesman.

"I guess it is a good deal," said Cindy. "All right, I'll buy it."

Writing

Look again at page 43. Then complete the salesman's lines.

Cindy: How much is the TV?

Salesman: It's $249.99.

Cindy: Wow! That's kind of expensive.

Salesman: It has stereo sound _____.

Cindy: I don't know.

Salesman: _____.

Cindy: Hmmmm . . . I still don't know.

Salesman: _____.

Cindy: That's nice, but I can't decide.

Salesman: _____.

The modal auxiliary *can*

Can is a modal auxiliary. **Can** means something is possible, or someone has the ability to do something.

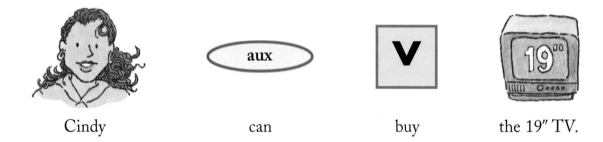

Cindy   can   buy   the 19″ TV.

We make the negative with the negative word **not.**

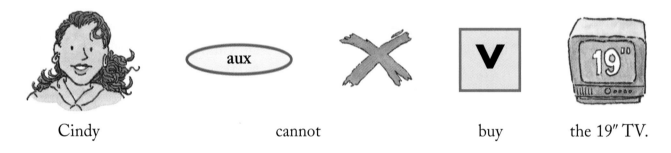

Cindy   cannot   buy   the 19″ TV.

We usually make a contraction.

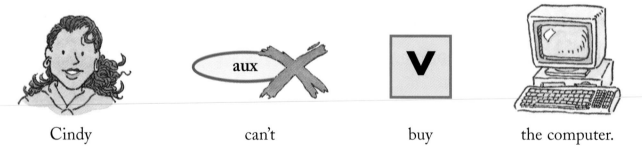

Cindy   can't   buy   the computer.

We make questions by changing the position of the subject and the modal auxiliary.

Can   Cindy   buy   the computer?

THE MODAL AUXILIARY CAN

I You He She We They	can cannot can't	buy	the 19-inch TV. the microwave. the computer.

YES/NO QUESTIONS

Can	I you he she we they	buy	the 19-inch TV the microwave the computer	?

SHORT (FORMAL) ANSWERS

Yes,	I you he she we they	can
No,		can't

•EXERCISE•

Look at the picture on page 37. Then complete these sentences with **can** or **can't.**

Mary Ann is shopping at a department store. She has $300.

1. She ___can't___ buy a video camera.

2. She _____ buy a microwave.

3. She _____ buy a keyboard.

4. She _____ buy a camera.

5. She _____ buy a stereo system.

6. She _____ buy a 25-inch TV.

7. She _____ buy an air conditioner.

8. She _____ buy a VCR.

9. She _____ buy a desktop computer.

10. She _____ buy a 19-inch TV.

Vocabulary

Do you know these words? Find them on page 37.

- ❑ 25-inch TV
- ❑ air conditioner
- ❑ microwave
- ❑ stereo system
- ❑ keyboard
- ❑ 19-inch TV
- ❑ video camera
- ❑ VCR
- ❑ camera
- ❑ desktop computer
- ❑ customer
- ❑ shopping cart
- ❑ money
- ❑ a fifty-dollar bill
- ❑ a hundred-dollar bill

Listening

Listen to your tape, and put your pictures in the correct places on your worksheet. Then check your answer on page 37.

Salesman:	Hi. Can I help you?
Mary Ann:	Yes. How much is the big TV?
Salesman:	The 25-inch one?
Mary Ann:	Yeah, that's the one.
Salesman:	That's five hundred and forty-nine dollars.
Mary Ann:	Five forty-nine! That's kind of expensive.
Salesman:	Well, we do have a 19-inch TV in stock.
Mary Ann:	How much is that?
Salesman:	Only two ninety-nine.
Mary Ann:	Wow. That's expensive, too.
Salesman:	It's an excellent TV.
Mary Ann:	Is that VCR on sale?
Salesman:	Yes, it's on special for one week only for two forty-nine.
Mary Ann:	Hmmmm. I just don't know.

How to

make a request using *can* or *may*

Can I leave at 8:30?

Sure.

May I have some paper, please?

Of course. Here you go.

Weather in the World

Moscow   **snowing**

**20°
cold**

Mexico City   **raining**

**70°
warm**

**Paris
partly cloudy**

**45°
cool**

Hong Kong   **cloudy**   **65°
warm**

foggy

New York

humid

smoggy

**90°
hot**

Lagos

sunny

windy

**85°
hot**

Focus On

- contrast simple present and present continuous tenses
- frequency adverbs
  always
  usually
  often

- describing the weather
- weather vocabulary
- how to discuss the weather

Ray is in Hong Kong on business.

110° F		hot
80° F		warm
60° F		cool
40° F		
20° F		cold
0° F		

100	
99	high
98	nineties
97	
96	mid-
95	nineties
94	
93	
92	low
91	nineties
90	

Listen

Listen and put your pictures in the correct places on your worksheet.

GROUP WORK

Practice asking and answering questions about temperature. Decide if the temperature is hot, warm, cool, or cold. Use your worksheet.

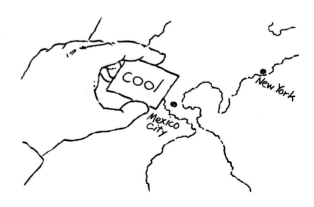

Reading

Read this, and put your pictures in the correct places on your worksheet.

> It's a beautiful day in Mexico City. The temperature is in the low eighties— a perfect day for the park.

> Good morning, Moscow. Be prepared. It's 15 degrees outside today—wear a warm jacket. And don't forget your gloves.

> Good afternoon. It's fifty-three degrees in downtown Paris.

Writing

Put your pictures on your worksheet to show the weather in five cities. Then complete the report below.

1. In ___New York___ it's ___65°___.

   It's ___warm_____.

2. In _____ it's ___°.

   It's _____.

3. In _____ it's ___°.

   It's _____.

4. In _____ it's ___°.

   It's _____.

5. In _____ it's ___°.

   It's _____.

Terry is in Moscow on business. She's calling her office in New York.

What's the weather like?

terrible/awful		so-so		pretty good		beautiful/wonderful
	not very good		OK		good/nice	

Listen and put your pictures in the correct places on your worksheet.

GROUP•WORK• Imagine you are in another city. Ask and answer questions like these. Use your worksheet.

Reading

Find each place on the maps. Then write words that describe the weather.

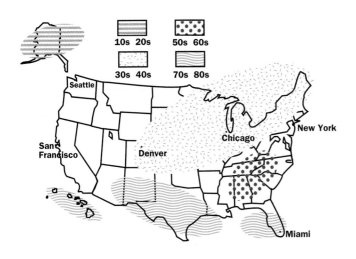

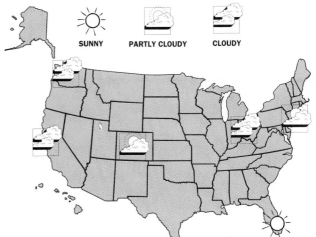

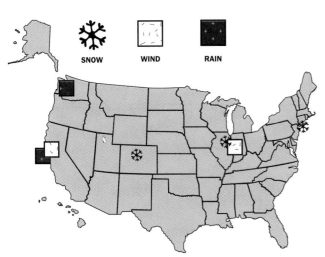

New York _cool, partly cloudy, snowing_.

Miami _____.

Chicago _____.

Seattle _____.

San Francisco _____.

Denver _____.

Writing

Use the words above to write weather reports for two of the cities.

_____

_____

_____

_____

Rita and Ken are talking about their countries.

Where are you from, Ken?

I'm from Tokyo, Japan.

What's the weather like in the summer in Tokyo?

It's usually hot and very humid.

		hot/warm. cool/cold. sunny/cloudy. smoggy. windy. foggy.
It's	always usually often	

It	rains snows	all the time. a lot. sometimes.

Listen

Listen and put your pictures in the correct places on your worksheet.

GROUP WORK

Ask the people in your group about the weather in different cities and countries. Use your worksheet.

What's the weather like in the winter in Mexico City?

It's usually cold. It's often smoggy.

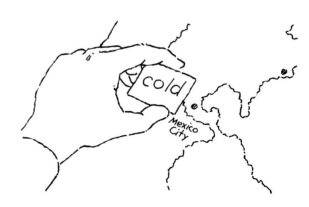

Reading

Read this, and put your pictures in the correct places on your worksheet.

JOSEPH'S SHOPPING TRIP

Joseph went shopping yesterday. He needed some sport shirts. He looked around, but he didn't see the sport shirts anywhere. He asked a salesperson.

"Excuse me," he said. "I'm looking for the men's sport shirts."

"They're over there, on the rack," said the salesperson.

Joseph looked. There were two racks.

"Which rack?," he asked.

"The rack on the right—under the clock," said the salesperson.

"Thanks," said Joseph.

Writing

Use your worksheet. Imagine you are in a department store. Where are these items? Write your answers below.

1. The shirts _____are on the rack under the clock_____.

2. The T-shirts _____.

3. The jeans _____.

4. The jackets _____.

5. The pants _____.

6. The shorts _____.

 *Read your sentences to the class. They will put their pictures in the correct places on their worksheets.*

Mike is at a new job in an office.

"Give this to Mr. Jones, please."

"Which person is Mr. Jones?"

"He's wearing a brown jacket and gray pants."

"Oh. OK."

He's wearing a red T-shirt and jeans.

She's wearing a pink-striped blouse and khaki pants.

 **Listen**

Listen and put your pictures in the correct places on your worksheet.

GROUP WORK

Practice questions and answers like these. Use your worksheet.

"What's he wearing?"

"He's wearing a brown jacket and gray pants."

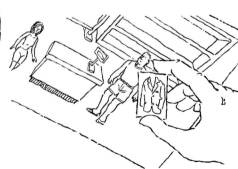

Reading/Writing

Read this, and label the pictures below.

high heels

Debbie and Joseph are trying on clothes.

How do the white shorts fit?

They're fine.

How does the plaid jacket fit?

It's too small.

How does the brown jacket fit?

It's too big.

How does [shirt] fit?

How do [shorts] fit?

Pants and shorts are always plural.

Listen

Listen and put your pictures in the correct places on your worksheet.

GROUP WORK

Practice questions and answers like these. Use your worksheet.

How do the gray pants fit on Joseph?

They're fine.

How do the black jeans fit on Debbie?

They're too big.

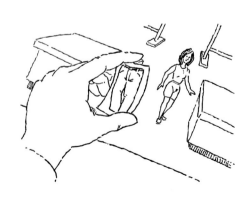

Reading

Read this, and put your pictures in the correct places on your worksheet.

DEBBIE'S SHOPPING TRIP

Debbie went shopping yesterday. She needed some blouses and pants. She found some pants on a rack to the left of the elevator. They were gray pants. They were too big for her. There were some khaki pants next to the gray pants. They fit fine, but Debbie didn't like them.

Debbie found some blouses on a sale table. There was a blue-and-orange-print blouse, but it was too big for her. There was a pink-striped blouse. The blouse fit her fine, but she didn't like it. In the end, Debbie didn't buy anything.

Writing

What are the people in your class wearing? Look around and write about them.

1. _____ is wearing _____
   _____ .

2. _____
   _____ .

3. _____
   _____ .

4. _____
   _____ .

5. _____
   _____ .

6. _____
   _____ .

Vince and Lori are getting dressed.

I have a job interview today.

What are you wearing?

I'm wearing my brown jacket and my gray pants.

That sounds good.

Listen

Listen and put your pictures in the correct places on your worksheet. Then check one of these places below.

Lori is going to ❑ the beach ❑ work
❑ a party

Practice questions and answers like these. Use your worksheet.

She's going to school. What's she wearing?

She's wearing _____ _____.

He's going to a party. What's he wearing?

He's wearing _____ _____.

Reading/Writing

Read this, and answer the questions below.

*Appropriate = correct; attire = clothes

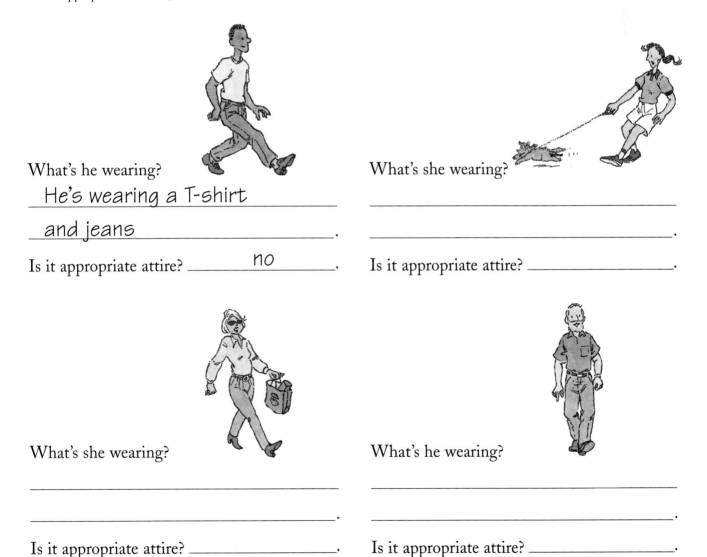

What's he wearing?

He's wearing a T-shirt

and jeans   .

Is it appropriate attire? _____ no _____.

What's she wearing?

_____

_____ .

Is it appropriate attire? _____.

What's she wearing?

_____

_____ .

Is it appropriate attire? _____.

What's he wearing?

_____

_____ .

Is it appropriate attire? _____.

Present continuous tense with future reference

We use the present continuous tense to describe something that is happening at this moment.

> He's wearing a brown jacket and gray pants.

We also use the present continuous tense to talk about the future.

> I'm wearing a brown jacket and gray pants.

We use **be + base form + -ing** to make the present continuous tense:

| I | am | working | future phrase tomorrow. |

We make questions like this:

| What | are | you | doing | future phrase tomorrow? |

When answering questions, we usually make contractions:

I'm working.

FUTURE WITH **GOING TO**

QUESTIONS

What	am	I	going to do	tomorrow? this Tuesday? next week?
	is	he she		
	are	we you they		

ANSWERS

I	am 'm 'm not	going to	go shopping. come to class. do the laundry. see a movie.
He She	is 's isn't		
We You They	are 're aren't		

SIMPLE PAST

QUESTIONS

What	did	I he she we you they	do	yesterday? last weekend? last Tuesday?

ANSWERS

I He She We You They	did didn't do	the laundry.
	went didn't go	dancing.
	came didn't come	to class.
	saw didn't see	a movie.

•EXERCISE•

Look at page 85. Then complete these sentences about Christina's schedule.

1. Tomorrow, Christina _____is going to go shopping_____.

2. Last Saturday, she _____.

3. This Saturday, _____.

4. Last Sunday, _____.

5. Last Monday, _____.

6. Next Thursday, _____.

7. Next Tuesday, _____.

Vocabulary

Do you know these words? Find them on page 85.

- ❏ the day before yesterday
- ❏ yesterday
- ❏ today
- ❏ tomorrow
- ❏ the day after tomorrow

- ❏ went to the doctor
- ❏ saw a movie
- ❏ did the laundry
- ❏ went dancing
- ❏ did the shopping

- ❏ going to go shopping
- ❏ going to go to a party
- ❏ going to go out to eat
- ❏ going to come to class

Listening

Listen to your tape, and put your pictures in the correct places on your worksheet. Then check your answer on page 85.

Victor:	Can you believe it's Wednesday already? What did you do last weekend?
Christina:	Good. I went dancing Sunday. Saturday, I just did the laundry. That wasn't much fun.
Victor:	How about last week? Did you do anything exciting?
Christina:	Let's see . . . last Wednesday, I saw a good movie.
Victor:	That's nice. Well, what are you going to do this week?
Christina:	Well, tomorrow I'm going to go shopping. And Saturday, I'm going to go to a party.
Victor:	You sure are busy! Are you going to come to class next Thursday?
Christina:	Of course, why do you ask?
Victor:	That's when we're going to have our final test.
Christina:	Oh, that's right.
Victor:	So what are you doing tonight? Would you like to go out to eat?
Christina:	No, I think I better stay home and study!

How to
apologize

Classic Movies

THEATER 1
NEXT SHOW 9:05

DRACULA
Starring
BELA LUGOSI

horror movie

THEATER 2
NEXT SHOW 8:50

RAIDERS of the LOST ARK
STARRING
HARRISON FORD

action movie

THEATER 3 ⇨
NEXT SHOW 9:40

A FISTFUL OF DOLLARS
STARRING
CLINT EASTWOOD

western

POP CORN

ZAP COLA

COMING SOON

THE 4 MARX BROTHERS
IN
DUCK SOUP

comedy

Beauty and the Beast

cartoon
color

title

CASABLANCA

drama
black & white
star

STARRING
HUMPHREY BOGART
AND INGRID BERGMAN
WITH PAUL HENREID

Focus On

- object pronouns
- past + **ago**
- talking about likes and dislikes
- movie vocabulary
- how to agree with someone

Matt and Sue are going to the movies.

Hi.

Good evening.

TICKETS
ADULTS   6.00
CHILDREN 3.00
SENIORS 3.00

What's playing in Theater 2?

Casablanca.

What kind of movie is that?

It's a drama with Humphrey Bogart.

OK. I'd like two tickets, please.

OK. Two tickets for Casablanca. That's twelve dollars.

Listen and put your pictures in the correct places on your worksheet.

GROUP·WORK

Practice asking and answering questions. Use your worksheet.

What's playing in Theater 1?

Dracula.

What kind of movie is that?

It's a horror movie.

WORKSHEET

NEXT SHOW! 9:05   THEATER

DRACULA

Reading

Read these ads. Then put your pictures in the correct places on your worksheet.

THEATER 1	THEATER 2	THEATER 3

THEATER 1

?

"The classic American movie about love, loss, war, and commitment."
Best Movies Guide

"Romantic. Exciting. Wonderful. Bogart is terrific!"
Movies On Video

THEATER 2

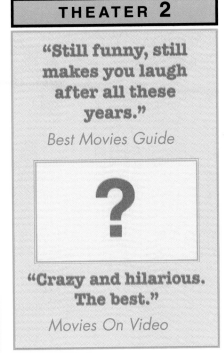

"Still funny, still makes you laugh after all these years."
Best Movies Guide

?

"Crazy and hilarious. The best."
Movies On Video

THEATER 3

"Thrilling, fun, exciting from beginning to end."
Best Movies Guide

?

"Very exciting. Has non-stop action and adventure."
Movies On Video

Writing

Complete these sentences about the movies above.

1. _____ is playing in Theater 1.

   It's _____.

2. _____ Theater 2.

   _____.

3. _____ Theater 3.

   _____.

Extra *Find some ads for movies in a newspaper. What words can you find from the ads above? What other words describe the movies?*

Ted wants to see Raiders of the Lost Ark.

Listen

Listen and put your pictures in the correct places on your worksheet.

GROUP·WORK

Practice asking and answering questions about movie times. Use your worksheet.

Reading

Read this, and put your pictures in the correct places on your worksheet.

WHAT'S AT THE CLASSIC TRIPLEX?

Casablanca   This is probably the most famous American drama ever made. It is a love story set in North Africa during World War II. It was made in 1942 and stars Humphrey Bogart and Ingrid Bergman. It's playing right now in Theater 2. (B&W)

Dracula   This is a classic horror movie, made in 1932. It stars Bela Lugosi as the vampire from Transylvania. It's coming next week. (B&W)

Duck Soup   This stars Groucho, Harpo, Chico, and Zeppo Marx —the Marx Brothers. Made in 1935, it is still funny today. Playing now in Theater 1. (B&W)

Raiders of the Lost Ark   This stars Harrison Ford as Indiana Jones, the hero who saves the world. There is lots of action and adventure. Playing now in Theater 3. (Color)

Writing

Write one sentence about each movie.

1. _Casablanca was made in 1942_____.

2. _____.

3. _____.

4. _____.

   *What is your favorite movie? Write four sentences about it, and read them to your group.*

Dracula *is playing in Theater 1. It starts at 9:05.*

When does *Dracula* start?
It starts in forty-five minutes.

When does *Dracula* start?
It's starting right now.

When does *Dracula* start?
It started ten minutes ago.

 Listen

Listen and put your pictures in the correct places on your worksheet.

GROUP WORK Pick a time. Then ask when the movies start. Put your pictures in the correct places on your worksheet.

Reading/Writing

Read this movie ad, and fill in the blanks next to it.

Star of the movie _____

Kind of movie _____

City _____

Phone number _____

First show _____

Is there parking? _____

Name of the theater _____

"**NON-STOP ACTION AND ADVENTURE**"
—Ronald Searle MOVIES MAGAZINE

Andre Demme

TOUGH TO KILL

PG-13

A story about a tough cop.

Garden City	Daily: 1:00, 3:20, 5:40, 8:10, 10:30
Acme Plaza	Sat & Sun MATINEE 12:00 (Noon)
330-1550	Free validated parking with ticket purchase

Work in groups. Write an ad for this movie.

_____
(quote)
— Ronald Searle MOVIES MAGAZINE

_____
(star)

_____
(name of movie)

A story about _____

_____

_____

_____

[rating]

Extra   *Use the newspaper. Find a drama, a comedy, an action movie,*
and a horror movie. Then decide which one you want to see.

Peter is talking about movies with Ann.

Do you like horror movies?

Yeah. I love them.

How about you?

No. I don't like them at all.

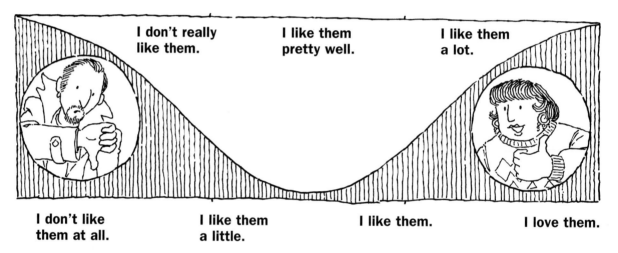

I hate them.

I don't really like them.

I like them pretty well.

I like them a lot.

I don't like them at all.

I like them a little.

I like them.

I love them.

Listen

Listen and put your pictures in the correct places on the chart above.

GROUP WORK

Ask your group questions like these. Then put your pictures in the correct places on the chart above.

Do you like horror movies?

No. I don't like them.

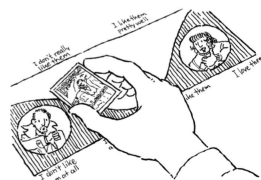

Reading

Read this, and complete the chart below.

FOREIGN MOVIES COMING TO THE ACME CLASSIC THEATER COMPLEX

Raise the Red Lantern   This film takes place in the 1920s. It's about a girl who marries a rich man. She becomes the rich man's fourth wife. It was directed by the famous Chinese director Zhang Yimou. 1991 (Color)

Like Water for Chocolate   This film is about a young woman who cannot marry the man she loves. She begins to cook, and her cooking becomes magical. Mexican director Alfonso Arau does a wonderful job. 1993 (Color)

The Seven Samurai   This classic Japanese movie is about seven swordsmen who fight bandits and protect a small village. Several American westerns copied this famous movie. 1954 (B&W)

War and Peace   This is the film version of the famous Russian novel. It's about life, love, and war in Russia in the 1800s. It took five years and a huge amount of money to make this movie. 1968 (Color)

NAME OF MOVIE				
COUNTRY				
YEAR MADE				
COLOR?				

Writing

Write about a famous movie from your country.

_____ is a famous movie from _____.
            name   *country*

It's about _____

_____

Object pronouns

The object in this sentence is **horror movies.**

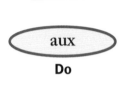
Do

you
(subject pronoun)

like

horror movies?
(object)

Them replaces the object. It is called an object pronoun.

I
(subject pronoun)

like

them
(object pronoun)

a little.

The object here is *Dracula.* It is singular (one thing).

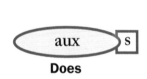
Does

Matt

like

Dracula?

The object pronoun for singular things is **it.**

He

likes

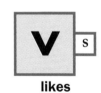
it

a lot.

Here are some other object pronouns.

I

like

him.

Matt

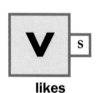
likes

me.

I

like

her.

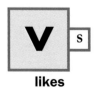
Sue

likes

you.

SIMPLE PRESENT TENSE

YES/NO QUESTIONS

Do	I you they	like	comedies? action movies? westerns? dramas?
Does	he she		

SHORT ANSWERS

Yes,	I you we they	do.
	he she	does.
No,	I you we they	don't.
	he she	doesn't.

•EXERCISE•

Complete these sentences with **it** or **them.**

1. Do you like horror movies? Yes, I like _____ a lot.

2. Did you like *Dracula?* Yeah, I liked _____ a lot.

3. How was *Duck Soup?* I didn't see _____. I was too late.

4. Did you see *Beauty and the Beast?* No, I don't like cartoons. I never go to _____.

5. Did you see *A Fistful of Dollars* on TV last night? No, but I saw _____ a long time ago.

6. I never see westerns. I just don't like _____.

7. *Casablanca* started fifteen minutes ago. We missed _____.

8. I rarely go to action movies. I don't like _____ a lot.

Extra   Read your writing from page 105 to the class. Your teacher
might want to collect all the different movies in a book.

Vocabulary

Do you know these words? Find them on page 97.

- ❏ theater
- ❏ next show
- ❏ a horror movie
- ❏ an action movie
- ❏ a western
- ❏ a comedy
- ❏ a drama
- ❏ a cartoon
- ❏ title
- ❏ star
- ❏ black & white
- ❏ color

Listening

Listen to your tape, and put your pictures in the correct places on your worksheet. Then check your answer on page 97.

Matt: Excuse me, when does *Raiders of the Lost Ark* start?

Clerk: In twenty minutes.

Matt: And what time is it now?

Clerk: It's eight-thirty.

Matt: Thanks a lot.

Sue: Is *Dracula* playing tonight?

Clerk: Yes, it is.

Sue: What time does it start?

Clerk: Uh, let's see...at nine-oh-five.

Sue: Thanks.

Peter: Excuse me, is *Duck Soup* playing tonight?

Clerk: No, I'm sorry. It's coming next week.

Peter: Oh, OK. Thanks.

Ann: Is that Arnold Schwarzenegger movie playing tonight?

Clerk: No, I'm sorry. That was last week.

Ann: Oh, darn it. Well, is the western, with Clint Eastwood...uh...I forget the name...playing tonight?

Clerk: Yes. It's in Theater 3.

Ann: Thanks.

How to
agree with someone

A Dream House

second story

swimming pool

first story

backyard

patio

garden

garage

porch

lot

front yard

trees

Focus On

- quantifiers
  - *much*
  - *many*
  - *a little*
  - *a few*

- house vocabulary

- stating a preference
  I would like a ...

- how to comment on good news and bad news

Karen and Neil are at a real estate office. They are looking for a house to rent.

This is a big, two-story house. It's got a swimming pool, too.

Does it have a garage?

Yes, it does. And it has a big front porch, too.

What's the rent?

It's eight hundred dollars a month.

Does it have	a pool? a garden? a garage?	It has It's got	a pool. a garden. a garage.	It's	small. big. one story. two story.

Listen

Listen and put your pictures in the correct places on your worksheet.

GROUP WORK

Practice asking and answering questions about a house. Use your worksheet.

It's a small, one-story house.

Yes. It's on the right side.

Does it have a garage?

WORKSHE...

Reading

Read this ad, and put your pictures in the correct places on your worksheet.

Come Visit Green Woods Estates,

a brand-new development of custom-built homes. These two-story homes are built on large, tree-shaded lots. Every home features a private backyard, with a swimming pool and a patio. All homes have a large traditional front porch and a two-car garage. Excellent schools.

2-5 bedrooms from $107,000.

GREEN WOOD ESTATES

Writing

Work alone or in a group. Write an ad for a new housing development. Give the development a name. Cut out a picture from a newspaper or magazine to use with your ad.

PLACE
PICTURE
HERE

Come visit _____ Estates. These _____ homes are

built on large, tree-shaded lots. Every home features _____

_____

_____

_____

_____

_____

Bruce is talking about his new house.

What's the house like?

It's small. It's just one story. But it's in a nice neighborhood. Very quiet.

Are there any trees in the yard?

Yeah. There are a lot of trees in the backyard, and there are a few trees on the left side of the house.

a lot of trees

some trees

a few trees

no trees

 Listen

Listen and put your pictures in the correct places on your worksheet.

GROUP WORK

Describe an imaginary house. Use your worksheet.

Yes, there are a few trees behind the house, and there are a lot of trees in front of the house.

Are there any trees?

WORKSHEET

Reading

Read this, and put your pictures in the correct places on your worksheet.

A NEW HOUSE

Mr. and Mrs. Lee saved their money for ten years. Then, they bought a new house. It cost $110,000. They paid $10,000 down and will pay $733.76 a month for thirty years. That's a long time, but the Lees don't care. They like their house a lot.

They especially like all the trees that surround their house. The house has a big garage on the left side. Next to the garage there are a lot of trees. The house also has a patio in the backyard. Behind the patio, there are some more trees. There are even a few trees in the front yard. There's a nice garden in front of the house with a lot of flowers. The Lees think that this is the nicest house they have ever lived in.

Writing

Read this, and then answer the questions below.

Mr. and Mrs. Lee are paying 8-percent interest on $100,000 for thirty years. They have an adjustable mortgage (the interest rate goes up and down). Here's a chart:

INTEREST RATE	MONTHLY PAYMENT
8.5%	$768.91
9.0%	$804.62
9.5%	$840.85
10.0%	$877.57

1. If the interest rate goes up to 8.5 percent, _they will pay $768.91 a month_

    _____.

2. If the interest rate goes up to 9.0 percent, _____

    _____.

3. If the interest rate goes up to 9.5 percent, _____

    _____.

4. If the interest rate goes up to 10.0 percent, _____

    _____.

Paul Kato is an architect. He's planning a house for Mr. and Mrs. Ramos.

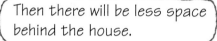

How do you like the plans?

I like them. But there's not much space in the front. I'd like a bigger front yard.

Then there will be less space behind the house.

Yes, I know. But I'd like a big front yard with lots of trees and room for a porch.

a lot of space　　　**some space**　　　**a little space not much space**　　　**no space**

Listen

Listen and put your pictures in the correct places on your worksheet.

GROUP WORK

Describe where the house is on the lot. Use the words above. Use your worksheet.

Is there any space between the house and the garage?

The garage is on the right.

There's a little space.

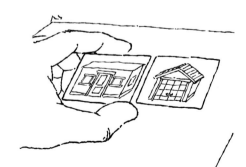

Reading/Writing

Read this, and then complete the writing exercise.

Colonial (1700–1820)
This is the classic "American" style. Colonial houses are usually a simple box shape. They have little decoration.

Spanish-style (1915–1940)
Buildings in this style usually have a tile roof and walls of stucco.

Greek Revival (1825–1860)
This style features porches with columns. This is a very popular style for libraries and government buildings.

Modern (1920–present)
Modern buildings usually have cement or stucco walls and flat roofs.

Split-level (1945–present)
A house in this style usually has a garage under a second story.

Victorian (1860–1910)
The Victorian style features porches, towers, and a lot of decoration.

Write four sentences about buildings in your neighborhood.
Example: There is a <u>modern</u> building <u>on Main Street, near Second Avenue.</u>

1. There is a _____ building _____

_____.

2. _____

_____.

3. _____

_____.

4. _____

_____.

Mr. and Mrs. Lim are building a new house. They are talking with an architect.

Listen and put your pictures in the correct places on your worksheet.

GROUP WORK

Pretend you are architects. Work with one person in your group and design a house. Use your worksheet.

Reading

The following story is from the novel *The House on Mango Street*, written by the Mexican-American writer Sandra Cisneros. Don't worry if you don't understand every word. Read this story, and label the picture below. Then ask your teacher about anything you didn't understand.

A HOUSE OF MY OWN   by Sandra Cisneros

Not a flat. Not an apartment in back. Not a man's house. Not a daddy's. A house all my own. With my porch and my pillow, my pretty purple petunias. My books and my stories. My two shoes waiting beside the bed. Nobody to shake a stick at. Nobody's garbage to pick up after.

Only a house quiet as snow, a space for myself to go, clean as paper before the poem.

"A House of My Own" by Sandra Cisneros from THE HOUSE ON MANGO STREET. Copyright ©1989 by Sandra Cisneros. Published in the United States by Vintage Books, a division of Random House, Inc., New York.

porch

Writing

Write a description of your dream house—the house you would like to live in someday.

I would like

Count and non-count quantifiers

Some nouns we can count. They can be singular or plural.

Some nouns we can't count. They are always a group, or a mass. They are always singular.

a tree   **13 trees**

space

We use **many** with count words and **much** with non-count or mass nouns.

How   **many**   **trees**   **are**   **there?**

How   **much**   **space**   **is**   **there?**

We use **a few** with count words and **a little** with non-count or mass nouns.

There   **are**   **a few**   **trees**   **next to the house.**

There   **is**   **a little**   **space**   **next to the house.**

We use **some, a lot of,** and **no** with both count words and non-count or mass nouns.

There are some trees.
There is some space.

There are a lot of trees.
There is a lot of space.

There are no trees.
There is no space.

COUNT AND NON-COUNT QUANTIFIERS

There is	a one	flower. tree. house.
There are	some a few a lot of no	flowers. trees. houses.

There is	some a little a lot of no	space. traffic. money.

QUESTIONS AND ANSWERS WITH **MUCH** AND **MANY**

How much	space traffic money	is	there?
How many	trees houses flowers	are	

There	is isn't	a lot. much.
	are aren't	a lot. many.

•EXERCISE•

Look at the picture on page 109. Fill in the blanks in these questions and answers about the picture.

1. How _____ *many* _____ trees are there in the backyard?

   _____ *There are a lot of trees* _____ .

2. How _____ space is there between the house and the garage?

   _____ .

3. How _____ trees are behind the pool?

   _____ .

4. How _____ trees are there in the front yard?

   _____ .

5. How _____ space is there between the house and the pool?

   _____ .

Vocabulary

Do you know these words? Find them on page 109.

- ❑ second story
- ❑ first story
- ❑ backyard
- ❑ front yard
- ❑ swimming pool
- ❑ patio
- ❑ porch
- ❑ trees
- ❑ garden
- ❑ garage

Listening

Listen to your tape, and put your pictures in the correct places on your worksheet. Then check your answer on page 109.

Valerie: How do you like your new house?

Karen: Oh, we love it. It's great!

Valerie: What's it like?

Karen: It's a big, two-story house, and there's a swimming pool on the left side of the house, and there's a garage on the right. Behind the swimming pool there are a few trees, so it's shady in the afternoon.

Valerie: Does it have a garden?

Karen: Yes, there's a garden between the garage and the house.

Valerie: Do you have a big backyard?

Karen: Yes. There's a lot of space back there. And there are a lot of trees in the backyard, too.

Valerie: It sounds great.

Karen: We like it a lot.

How to

comment on good news and bad news

Verb Charts

base form	past form	continuous form	meaning in your language
be (am/is/are)	was/were	being	
add	added	adding	
answer	answered	answering	
arrive	arrived	arriving	
ask	asked	asking	
borrow	borrowed	borrowing	
bring	brought	bringing	
build	built	building	
buy	bought	buying	
call	called	calling	
change	changed	changing	
check	checked	checking	
clarify	clarified	clarifying	

base form	past form	continuous form	meaning in your language
V	**V** P	**V** ing	
come	came	coming	
comment	commented	commenting	
complete	completed	completing	
connect	connected	connecting	
continue	continued	continuing	
cook	cooked	cooking	
cross	crossed	crossing	
cry	cried	crying	
dance	danced	dancing	
describe	described	describing	
dig	dug	digging	
discuss	discussed	discussing	
do	did	doing	
drink	drank	drinking	
eat	ate	eating	
exercise	exercised	exercising	

base form	past form	continuous form	meaning in your language
expect	expected	expecting	
find	found	finding	
finish	finished	finishing	
fit	fit	fitting	
forget	forgot	forgetting	
form	formed	forming	
get	got	getting	
get on	getting on	got on	
get off	getting off	got off	
give	gave	giving	
go	went	going	
guess	guessed	guessing	
hate	hated	hating	
happen	happened	happening	
have	had	having	
hold	held	holding	

base form	past form	continuous form	meaning in your language
hug	hugged	hugging	
imagine	imagined	imagining	
introduce	introduced	introducing	
invite	invited	inviting	
kiss	kissed	kissing	
know	knew	knowing	
label	labeled	labeling	
lay	laid	laying	
leave	left	leaving	
lend	lent	lending	
like	liked	liking	
listen	listened	listening	
live	lived	living	
look	looked	looking	
love	loved	loving	
make	made	making	

base form	past form	continuous form	meaning in your language
		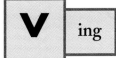	
measure	measured	measuring	
open	opened	opening	
pack	packed	packing	
pay	paid	paying	
plan	planned	planning	
plant	planted	planting	
play	played	playing	
plug	plugged	plugging	
point	pointed	pointing	
practice	practiced	practicing	
put	put	putting	
rain	rained	raining	
read	read	reading	
relax	relaxed	relaxing	
remember	remembered	remembering	
rent	rented	renting	

base form	past form	continuous form	meaning in your language
	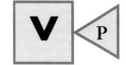	V ing	
repeat	repeated	repeating	
request	requested	requesting	
save	saved	saving	
say	said	saying	
see	saw	seeing	
sells	sold	selling	
shop	shopped	shopping	
show	showed	showing	
sit	sat	sitting	
sleep	slept	sleeping	
snow	snowed	snowing	
speak	spoke	speaking	
star	starred	starring	
start	started	starting	
state	stated	stating	
study	studied	studying	

base form	past form	continuous form	meaning in your language
take	took	taking	
talk	talked	talking	
tell	told	telling	
think	thought	thinking	
turn	turned	turning	
underline	underlined	underlining	
use	used	using	
visit	visited	visiting	
want	wanted	wanting	
watch	watched	watching	
wear	wore	wearing	
work	worked	working	
write	wrote	writing	

Dialogues

Listen CHAPTER 1
A Living Room

Situation A, page 2

Narrator: These people from the Quick Moving Company have come to help move furniture.

A: Yes?

B: Quick Moving Company, (Ma'am/Sir).

A: Hi. Come in.

B: Where do you want this table, (Ma'am/Sir)?

A: Put it on the left side of the living room, please.

B: Okay.

C: Hi. Where do you want the sofa?

A: Put it against the far wall. Under the window there.

B: How about this armchair?

A: Put it on the right side of the room.

B: Over here?

A: Yes, that's fine.

Situation B, page 4

Narrator: This person is asking a friend about his/her living room.

A: Is there a sofa in your living room?

B: Yeah. It's on the right.

A: How about an armchair, _(name)_ ? Do you have one?

B: Uh-huh. It's against the far wall.

A: Is there an end table in your living room?

B: Yes, there is. It's against the far wall, to the right of the armchair.

A: Is there a lamp in your living room?

B: Yes. It's on the end table.

Situation C, page 6

Narrator: These people are describing their new apartments to a friend.

A: I got a new apartment.

B: Really? What's it like?

A: It's great. There are three windows, so it's really sunny. One window is on the right as you walk in, and the other two are in the far wall. My sofa is in front of the two windows, and in the morning it's a good place to sit and read.

Narrator: Clear your worksheet and listen again.

A: Do you want to hear about my new apartment?

B: Sure! What's it like?

A: Well, it's in a nice neighborhood. And it's cheap. But the living room is kind of dark. There's only one window, on the left. And the window is pretty small.

B: Do you have a lot of furniture in your living room?

A: Not really. There's a couch that folds out into a bed on the left side of the room, and a large table on the right. I put my TV on the table.

B: That sounds big enough to me.

A: I guess it is, at least for now.

Situation D, page 8

Narrator: This person is talking about the past.

A: When I was a small child, our living room was big. There were four windows—two windows on the right side and two windows in the far wall. It was very sunny. There was a big sofa under the windows in the far wall. And next to the sofa, on the left, there was a small table. There was always candy in a bowl on that small table.

Getting Around

Situation A, page 14

Narrator: These people are calling for directions to the places they need to go.

A: Good afternoon, A and B Hardware Store.
B: Yes. How late are you open today?
A: We're open till nine o'clock tonight, (Ma'am/Sir).
B: Oh, good. And where are you located?
A: We're on Second Street near the corner of Lincoln Avenue. We're across from the museum.
B: OK. Thanks a lot.

A: Good morning, John F. Kennedy Elementary School.
B: Hi, this is Acme Shipping. We have a delivery for you. Where are you located exactly?
A: We're on Third Street. North of Lincoln. We're right across from the library.
B: OK. On Third Street. North of Lincoln. Across from the library.
A: That's correct.

Situation B, page 16

Narrator: This person is asking for directions. Look on your worksheet. The car is on Second Street, south of Washington Boulevard. Do you see it? Now listen and put Crown Computers in the correct place on your worksheet.

A: Excuse me, how do you get to Crown Computers?
B: Crown Computers? I don't know. Never heard of it.
A: Excuse me, how do you get to Crown Computers?
C: Crown Computers? Let's see....Go down this street, and take a right up there at Washington Boulevard. Go one block and turn left on Third Street. It's on your right, just past the highway exit.

A: I'm sorry. Could you repeat that?
C: Sure. You go down this street, and then you take a right up there at Washington Boulevard. Go down one block and then turn left on Third Street. It's on your right, just past the highway exit.
A: Thanks so much.
C: You're welcome.

Situation C, page 18

Narrator: This person is driving to the store and calls in order to get directions.

A: How do I get to your store?
B: Where are you coming from?
A: From Farmdale. On the highway.
B: OK. Get off the highway at exit 3. Go right on Third Street, then take a quick left. That's Lincoln. Go down two blocks, and we're on the right.
A: I'm sorry. Could you repeat that, please?
B: You get off the highway at exit 3. Then go right on Third Street. Uh, then take a quick left. Now you're on Lincoln. Go down two blocks, and we're on the right. Across the street from the supermarket.
A: Thank you very much.

Situation D, page 20

Narrator: This person is describing where he/she lives.

A: Where do you live, _(name)_ ?
B: On second Street, at the corner of Lincoln.
A: That big house?
B: No, it's an apartment. It's across the street from the house, on the northeast corner.
A: That's a nice neighborhood.
B: Yeah. The museum's right down the street. And there's a police station one block away on the corner of Lincoln and First, so it's really safe.

Listen CHAPTER 3
Likes and Dislikes

Situation A, page 26

Narrator: These people are talking about what they like to do on weekends.

A: What do you like to do on the weekends, _(name)_ ?

B: I kind of like to go to the movies. And I love to play all kinds of sports.

A: Do you like to go shopping?

B: No, not very much.

Narrator: Clear your worksheet and listen again.

B: Do you like to go shopping, _(name)_ ?

A: Yeah, quite a bit. But my favorite thing is dancing. I love to go dancing.

Situation B, page 28

Narrator: These people are talking about their likes and dislikes.

A: Tell me about yourself, _(name)_ .

B: Well, I really like to cook, especially French food. But I don't like to watch TV very much.

A: How about sports and exercise?

B: I kind of like to play sports, but I don't like to exercise—in fact, I _hate_ to exercise. My favorite thing to do in my free time is read. I _love_ to read. I read all the time.

Situation C, page 30

Narrator: This person is answering questions about his/her free time.

A: Do you ever go shopping?

B: Sometimes. I don't like it that much. But playing basketball—that's different. I play basketball all the time.

C: All the time? Every day?

B: Practically. At least five times a week.

D: Do you ever watch TV?

B: Yeah. I watch TV a lot. Pretty much every night.

Situation D, page 32

Narrator: A group of people asks a friend about her/his free time.

A: How often do you go to the movies, _(name)_ ?

B: Oh, maybe three times a year.

C: That's not very often.

D: How often do you play basketball, _(name)_ ?

B: Never.

A: How about watching TV? How often do you do that?

B: Usually every day.

C: That's a lot.

Buying Things

Situation A, page 38

Narrator: These people are shopping in the electronics section of a busy department store.

A: Good afternoon, (Ma'am/Sir). Are you looking for anything in particular?

B: That video camera over there …

A: This one?

B: Yeah. How much is it?

A: The camera is on sale for $899. It's really a fine piece of equipment.

B: Can I take a look at it?

A: Sure. Here.

A: Hi. Can I help you?

B: Yes. How much is that keyboard over there? The big one.

A: The big one is a Yamaha. It's five ninety-nine.

B: Can I play it?

A: Sure. Just a minute.

Situation B, page 40

Narrator: In the department store, these two friends are looking at VCRs together.

A: Hi. Can I help you?

B: How much is the VCR?

A: It's two forty-nine.

B: OK. Hey *(name)*, can I borrow fifty dollars?

C: Fifty dollars?

B: Yeah. Just until Friday?

C: Can you pay me back on Friday?

B: Uh-huh. I promise.

C: OK. here.

B: Thanks a lot.

Situation C, page 42

Narrator: How much money does Frank have?

A: Frank can't buy the air conditioner or the video camera because he doesn't have enough money, but he can buy the 19-inch TV and the microwave. How much money does he have?

Situation D, page 44

Narrator: This salesperson in the electronics department is helping this shopper decide what to buy.

A: Hi. Do you need help with something?

B: How much is that big stereo system?

A: Oh, that's a nice system—it's two ninety-nine.

B: Wow! That's pretty expensive.

A: Not really, it's an excellent system. It has a very good CD player, and the speakers are good too.

B: I don't know …

A: Actually, it's on special this week. It's usually three-fifty.

B: I don't know. It's a lot more than I wanted to spend.

A: But it's a very good buy.

B: Let me think about it.

Weather Around the World

Situation A, page 50

Narrator: These people are talking on the phone about the weather.

A: Hi, *(name)* . How's everything back in New York?

B: OK here in the office, but it's really cold outside. It's in the low twenties. It was twenty two degrees this morning.

A: Wow, you poor thing! Well, I hate to tell you, but it's beautiful here in Buenos Aires. Warm, clear, sunny—about 72 degrees right now.

B: Boy, are you lucky!

A: Hi, *(name)* . How are things in Paris?

B: OK. The weather is kind of cool—probably about 50 degrees right now.

A: You're lucky! It's so hot in Mexico City right now. It's at least 100 degrees in the shade. Awful weather!

Situation B, page 52

Narrator: This person is talking on the phone to a friend in New York City.

A: Hello, *(name)* ?

B: Yes, hi *(name)* . Are you calling from Paris?

A: No. That was yesterday. I'm in Hong Kong today.

B: Hong Kong? How's the weather there?

A: Terrible. It's raining really hard, and it's very windy. It's in the low forties. Just terrible. How's New York?

B: Good … perfect fall weather. It's sunny, cool, clear. Just fine.

A: I wish I could be there!

Situation C, page 54

Narrator: These two people are talking about the weather in their home countries.

A: Where are you from, *(name)* ?

B: I'm from Moscow.

A: What's the weather like in Moscow in the winter?

B: It's usually very cold. It snows a lot. How about you, *(name)* ?

A: I'm from a small town near Buenos Aires.

B: What's the weather like in the winter there?

A: It's usually warm and it rains a lot.

Situation D, page 56

Narrator: These people are talking about the past.

A: I left Buenos Aires six months ago. I remember the day I left. It was cool and windy—unusual weather for that season. It made me feel even sadder.

B: I left Hong Kong about a year ago. It was very, very hot—in the nineties and humid too. I remember I was glad to get on the airplane where it was cool.

C: I left Paris … let's see … about three years ago. It was a beautiful day. Warm and very sunny. Clear. Paris looked so beautiful—I didn't want to go.

The Job Site

Situation A, page 62

Narrator: These people are construction workers. They are talking to their boss.

A: OK. First we have to lay bricks for a patio.
B: Where does it go?
A: Five feet to the left of the house.
B: Five feet to the left? OK.
A: We also have to dig a hole for the tree.
C: Where do you want that?
A: Let' see. … uh, that goes ten feet to the right of the house.
C: Ten feet?
A: Uh-huh. Over there on the right side.

Situation B, page 64

Narrator: This worker is talking to the boss on the car phone.

A: How's the job going?
B: Good. Dave is laying the bricks for the patio right now.
A: That's ten feet to the left of the house, right?
B: That's right. Ten feet.
A: Good. How's the fence going?
B: Fine. Lucy and Dave are working on that. Let me just make sure—the fence is only seven feet in front of the house, right?
A: Yeah, that's right.

Situation C, page 66

Narrator: This worker is talking to the boss on the car phone again.

A: Did you finish the garden?
B: Yes. It's all done. Ten feet to the right of the house. It looks good.
A: Good. Did you finish the fences?
B: We finished one of them. We finished the fence on the left side of the house, but we didn't finish the one in front of the house. Lucy and Phil are working on the one in the front right now.
A: OK. Sounds good. Keep working.
B: I'll talk to you later.
A: Yeah. See ya.

Situation D, page 68

Narrator: These neighbors meet in the street.

A: _(name)_ ! Hi. How are you?
B: Fine. How are you? How's the family?
A: Good. We've been pretty busy. We just had a lot of work done on the house.
B: Really? What kind of work?
A: Well, we put a brick patio next to the house. You know, under that big tree on the left?
B: Big tree?
A: Yeah. Right next to the house, on the left. Just a couple of feet from the house. It's a big oak.
B: Oh, yeah, I remember that tree. Oh, that sounds great. A patio?
A: Yeah, it's really nice. A big brick one. We have chairs and a table out there.
B: That sounds great!

Clothing

Situation A, page 74

Narrator: These people are shopping for clothes.

A: Hi. Can I help you with something?
B: Yeah. I'm looking for the blue jeans.
A: They're over there, on the shelf.
B: Which shelf?
A: The one near the elevator. Your size would probably be on the middle shelf.
B: Thanks a lot.

A: Excuse me.
B: Sure. What can I help you with?
A: Where are the shorts?
B: Most of them are on that rack over there.
A: Which one?
B: The one in front of the exit over there.

Situation B, page 76

Narrator: These people are describing other people at work. They are talking about the clothes that their co-workers are wearing.

A: This package goes to Mr. Carlton.
B: Which one is he?
A: See the guy over there wearing the wild sports shirt and the black jeans? That's him.

A: This is for Ms. Jackson.
B: Which woman is that?
A: She's wearing a plaid jacket and khaki pants.
B: OK. I see her.

Situation C, page 78

Narrator: These people are in the department store trying on clothes.

A: What are you trying on (female name)?
B: This print shirt. It's really neat—it's like a Hawaiian shirt.
A: Does it fit OK?
B: No. It's way too big.

A: How do the gray pants fit (male name)?
B: They're fine, but this plaid jacket is way too small.

Situation D, page 80

Narrator: This person is giving a friend advice about what to wear on an important day.

A: I'm really nervous about today.
B: Oh, you'll be fine.
A: I'm wearing my new plaid jacket and khakis. What do you think?
B: Hmmm. I don't know. Maybe something a little more conservative would be better.
A: You think so?
B: Yeah. After all, you want to make a good impression with your boss, don't you?

The Calendar

Situation A, page 86

Narrator: This person is calling the doctor's office to make an appointment.

A: Hello, Dr. Martin's office.

B: Hi. This is _(name)_ . I'd like to make an appointment with the doctor.

A: OK. Let's see. … how about this Thursday?

B: No, I'm sorry. I'm busy this Thursday.

A: We have an opening on Friday, in the afternoon.

B: No, afternoons are no good. Do you have anything in the morning?

A: Not until next Tuesday. Is that OK?

B: Next Tuesday is fine.

A: OK. How about next Tuesday at 10 o'clock?

B: That's fine.

A: Great. We'll see you then.

B: OK, thanks. Bye.

A: Bye now.

Situation B, page 88

Narrator: These people are saying goodbye on a Friday.

A: So long, _(name)_ . Have a good weekend. What are you going to do? Anything exciting?

B: No, not really. Saturday I'm going to do the shopping and do my laundry.

A: Just your shopping and laundry?

B: Yeah. How about you?

A: I'm going to see a movie tonight.

B: What movie?

A: Hmm … I can't remember the name. It's an action movie.

Situation C, page 90

Narrator: These friends are talking on a Monday.

A: Hi, _(name)_ . How are you doing?

B: Fine. Did you have a good weekend? What did you do?

A: Yeah, it was pretty good. I went out to eat Saturday night with some friends.

B: What kind of food did you have?

A: Chinese food. I love Chinese food. How about you? What did you do?

B: I went to a movie Friday night. And I went dancing Saturday night.

A: That sounds great!

B: Yeah. It was a pretty good weekend.

Situation D, page 92

Narrator: It's Friday, and these friends are discussing their weekend plans.

A: Have a good weekend, _(name)_ .

B: Thanks, you too! What are you going to do this weekend?

A: Saturday, I'm going to go shopping. I need some new socks. How about you?

B: I'm going to go to a party Saturday night. It's a birthday party for my cousin.

A: That sounds nice. Have a good time!

B: Thanks, you too. See you later.

A: Yeah, see you.

Narrator: Clear your worksheet and listen again. It's now Monday, and two different friends are talking.

A: Did you have a good weekend _(name)_ ? What did you do?

B: Nothing much. I did my laundry on Saturday and on Sunday I did the shopping. That's it.

A: I didn't have a good weekend, either. I was sick all weekend. I went to the doctor last Friday. He said it was the flu.

B: Are you OK now?

A: Yeah. I'm better today.

CHAPTER 9

Classic Movies

Situation A, page 98

Narrator: This telephone message tells what movies are playing at the local movie theater.

A: Hi, you have reached Movie World, the place to go to see classic movies, and only classic movies. This week, in Theater 2, we have the classic horror movie, *Dracula,* starring Bela Lugosi as the vampire. If you like westerns, in Theater 1 we are showing *A Fistful of Dollars,* starring Clint Eastwood. And especially for the kids, in Theater 3 we have the wonderful Disney cartoon, *Beauty and the Beast.*

Situation B, page 100

Narrator: This theater employee is answering a lot of questions about the movies.

A: Is *Duck Soup* playing tonight?
B: Uh-huh.
A: What time does it start?
B: The next show is at 9:40.
A: Thank you, I'll take two tickets, please.
C: Hi. Is *A Fistful of Dollars* playing tonight?
B: No, it's coming next week.
C: Oh, hmm … well what is playing?
B: *Raiders of the Lost Ark* and *Duck Soup.*
C: What time does *Raiders of the Lost Ark* start?
B: 9:05 is the next show.
C: Great, I'll take two tickets, please.

Situation C, page 102

Narrator: This theater employee is answering a lot of questions about the movies.

B: Next, please. Hi, welcome to Film World. Can I help you.
A: Uh, yeah … what time is it now?
B: It's 8:45.
A: And when does *Duck Soup* start?
B: It starts in five minutes.
A: Great. I'll take two tickets, please.

──────────

B: Welcome to Film World. Do you want tickets for *Duck Soup?*
A: No, I don't like comedies. What time is it anyway?
B: 9:15.
A: When does *Beauty and the Beast* start?
B: I'm sorry. It started 10 minutes ago.
A: Oh, darn it. What about *A Fistful of Dollars?* When does it start?
B: It starts at 9:40.
A: OK, I'll take one ticket to that, please.

Situation D, page 104

Narrator: These friends are talking about what movie they want to see.

A: What movie to you want to see tonight? *Raiders of the Lost Ark* is playing. Do you like action movies?
B: I like them a little. I really love comedies though. Are any comedies playing?
A: No, not tonight. How about horror movies? *Dracula* is playing.
B: No. I don't really like horror movies at all.
A: Do you like westerns?
B: Pretty well. What's playing?
A: *A Fistful of Dollars* with Clint Eastwood.
B: OK, that sounds good. Let's go to that.

A Dream House

Situation A, page 110

Narrator: This real estate agent tells a customer about a house.

A: This house has one story, but it's quite big. It has a patio on the right side of the house and a big pool in front of the patio.

B: Does it have a garage?

A: Yes. On the other side of the house. Over on the left.

B: How about a porch?

A: No, it doesn't have a porch.

B: Does it have a garden?

A: Yes. In the front yard there's a very nice garden.

Situation B, page 112

Narrator: This person is describing his/her yard to a friend.

A: We bought a new house.

B: Really? That's great. What's it like?

A: It's only one story, and it's pretty small, but it's OK for just the two of us.

B: What's the yard like? Are there any trees?

A: There are some trees in the side yard, to the left of the house. And there are a few in the back yard, too.

B: It sounds really nice.

A: Yes, it is. We're very happy with it.

Situation C, page 114

Narrator: This architect is discussing the plans for a new house with a client.

A: So, how do you like the plans?

B: I like them. But there's a lot of space in front of the house. That's a very big front yard. Is that necessary?

A: Well, it's a good place for a garden. See, you can put a big garden right there, in front of the porch. And then there's still a lot of space between the house and the street, so the house won't be so noisy. Also, there are some trees in the front yard now, and I think if we keep the trees there it will cut down the noise.

B: Yeah, you're probably right. But what about the garage? Where will it go?

A: Oh, I forgot to put it in this plan. I thought it would go to the right of the house. See? There's plenty of room.

Situation D, page 116

Narrator: This person is discussing plans for a new house with an architect.

A: Do you want one story or two stories?

B: Well, it's just the two of us. We don't need that much space. I guess one story would be fine.

A: OK. How about a garage?

B: Yeah. I definitely want a garage. We have two cars.

A: How much space do you want between the house and the garage?

B: Just a little. No, actually, none at all.

A: No space? So you want them connected?

B: Yeah. I think it's better if the house and the garage are connected.

A: But what about the porch? Didn't you tell me you wanted a porch?

B: Yes, but I've changed my mind. Maybe a nice patio behind the house instead.

A: We can do that. And look, there will still be enough room for a small garden right behind the patio.

B: Great! I love fresh vegetables.

WORKSHEET

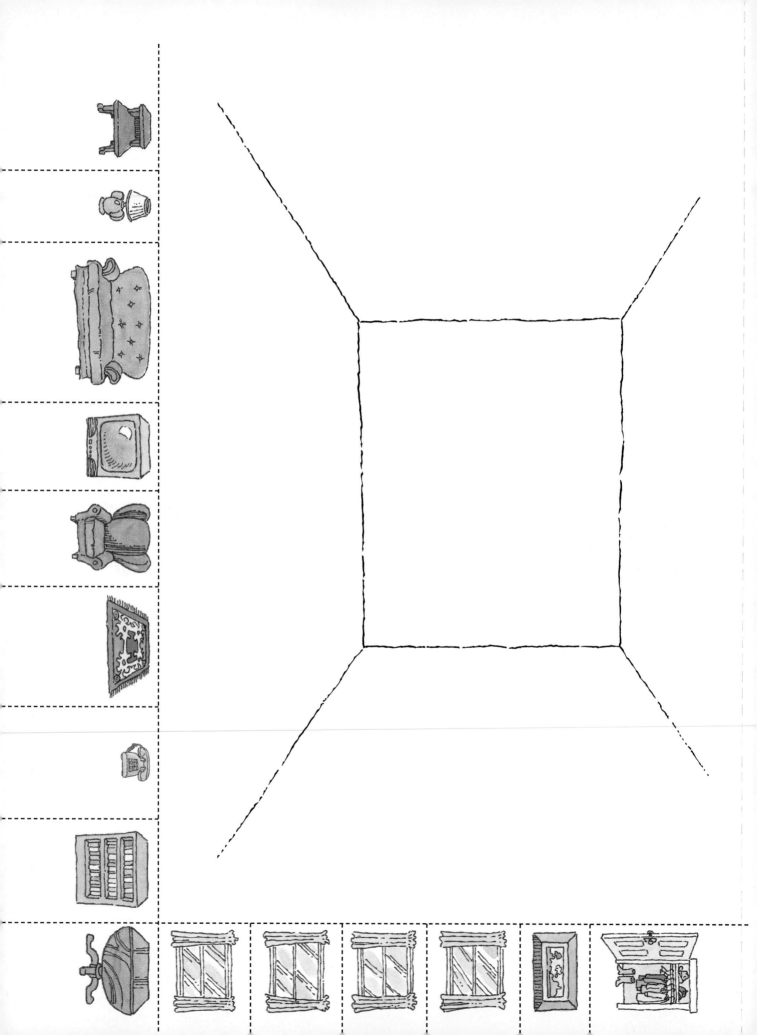

WORKSHEET

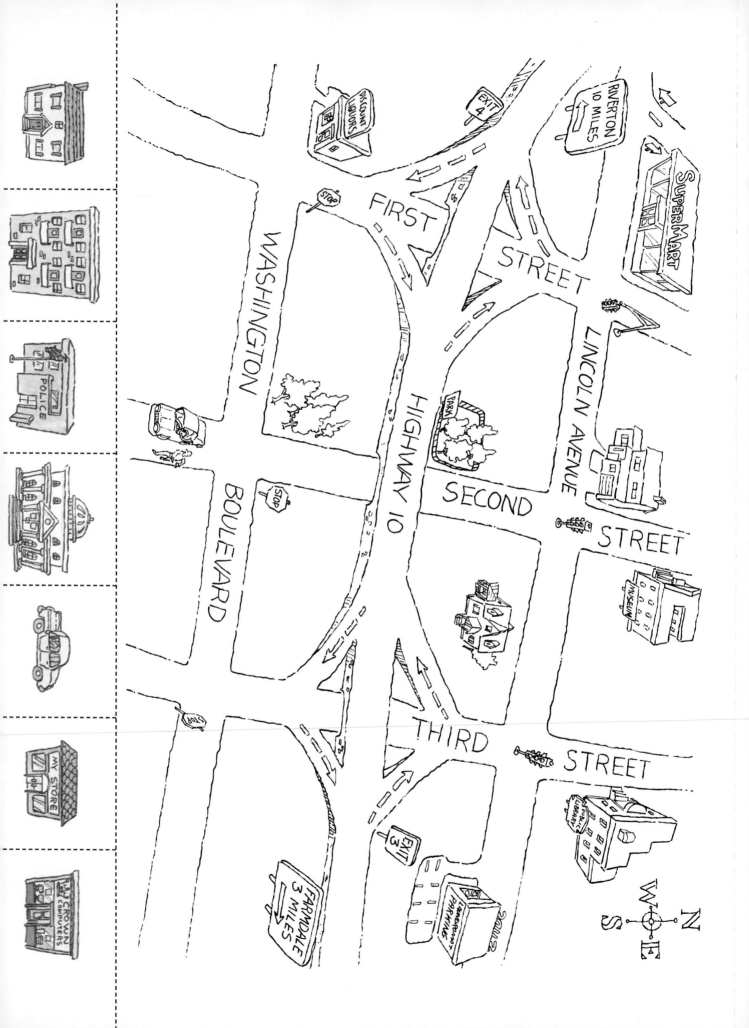

WORKSHEET

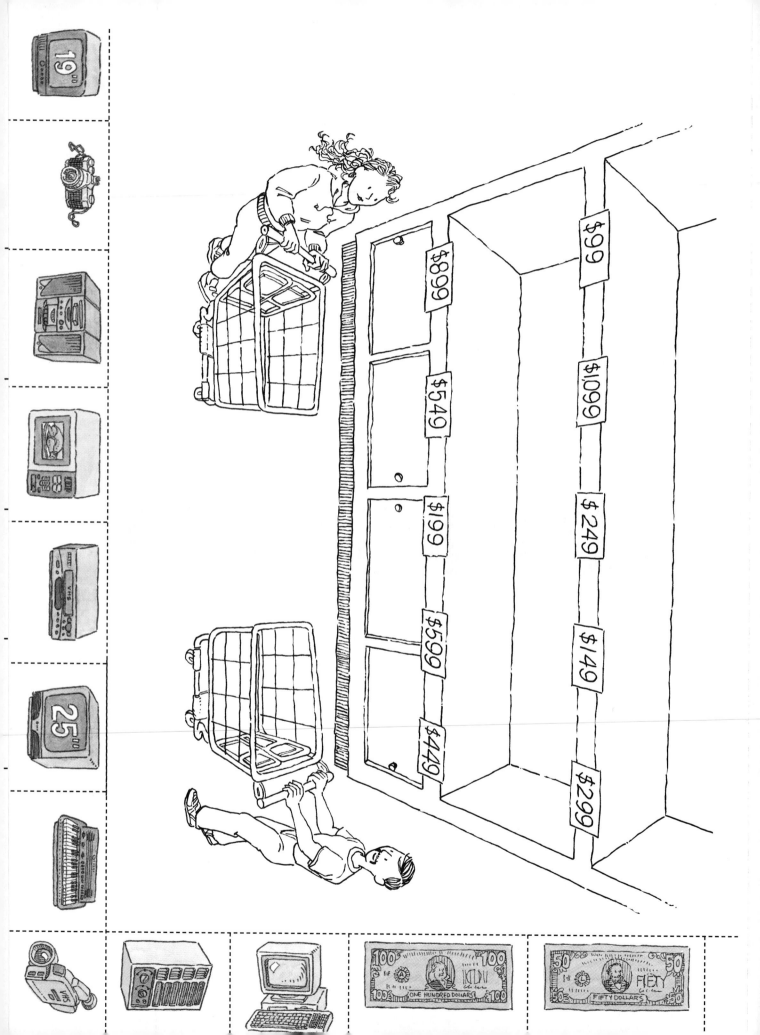

WORKSHEET

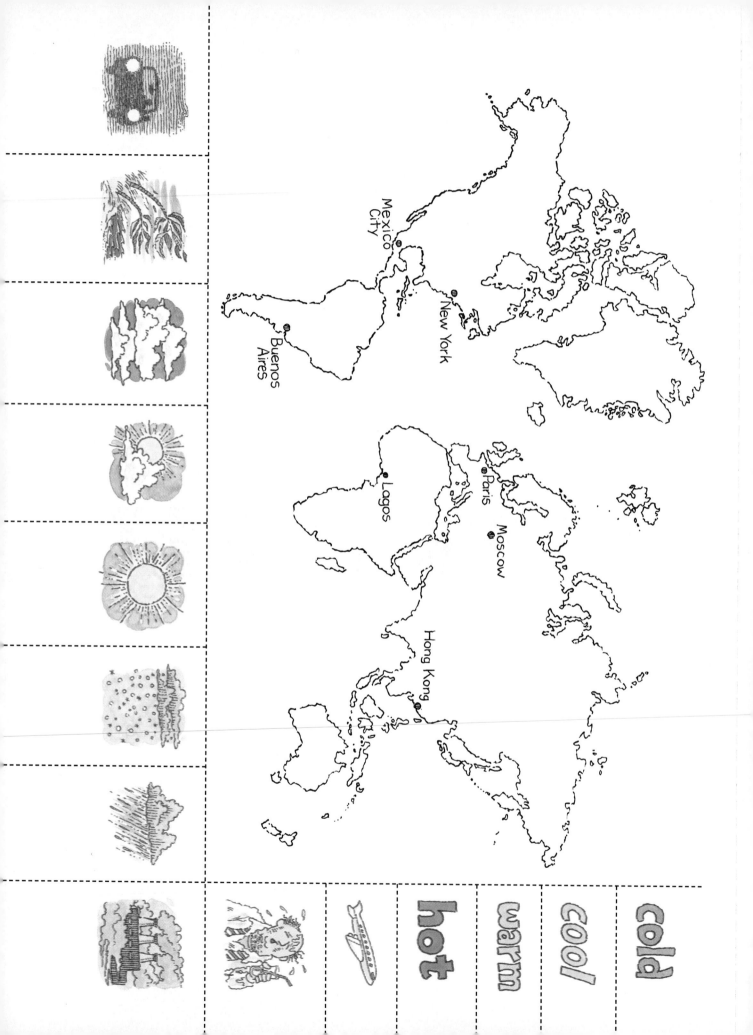

Mexico City

New York

Buenos Aires

Lagos

Paris

Moscow

Hong Kong

hot

warm

cool

cold

WORKSHEET

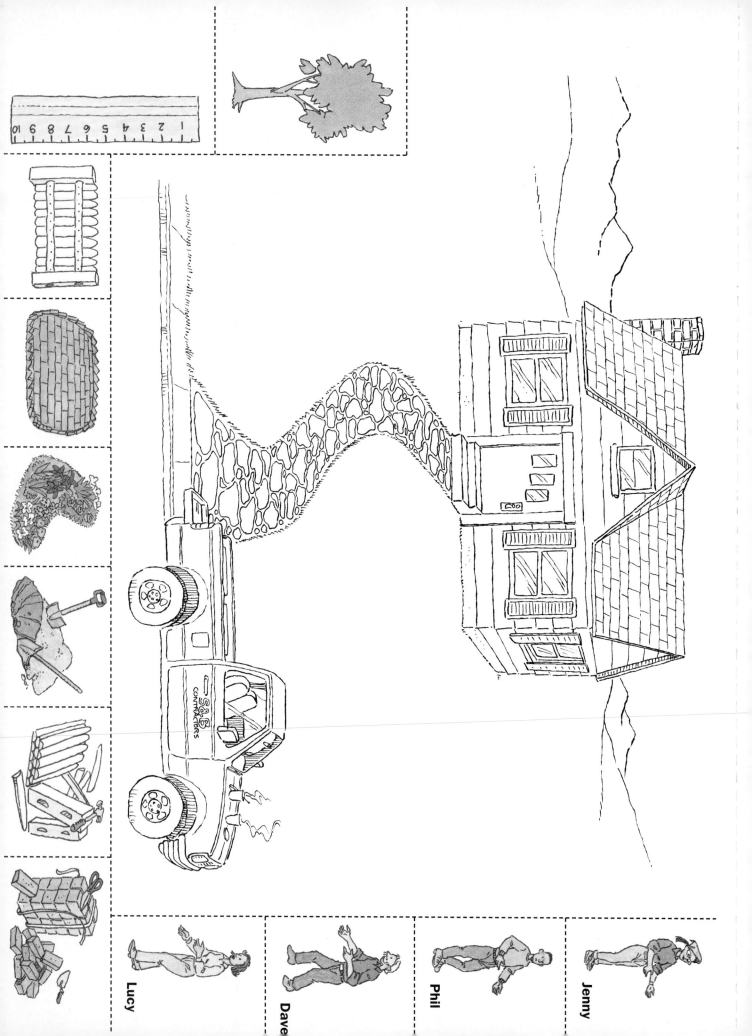

Lucy

Dave

Phil

Jenny

WORKSHEET

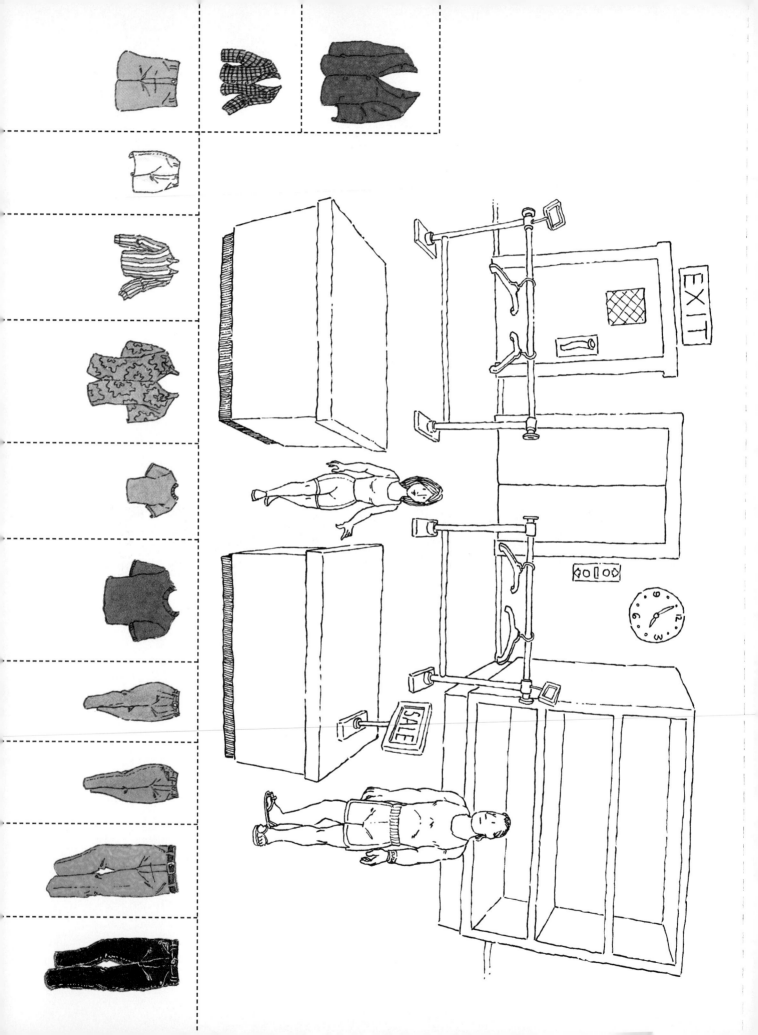

WORKSHEET

Note to Instructor: Have students fill in the calendar with the current dates

Sunday	Monday	Tuesday	Wednesday	Thursday	Friday	Saturday

WORKSHEET

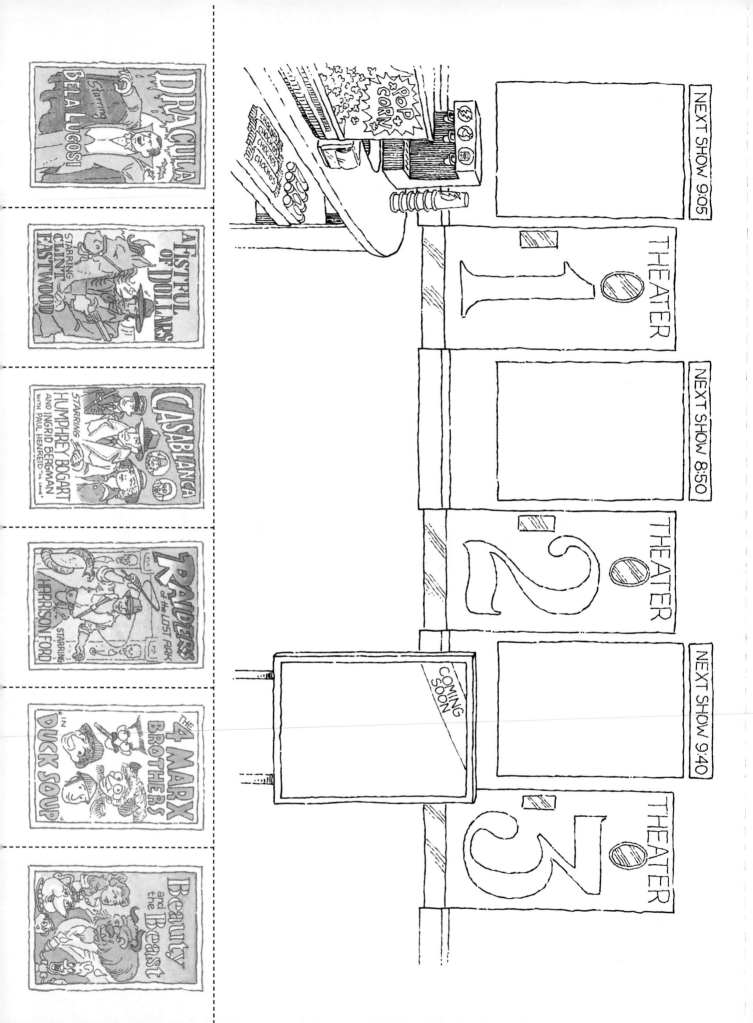

WORKSHEET

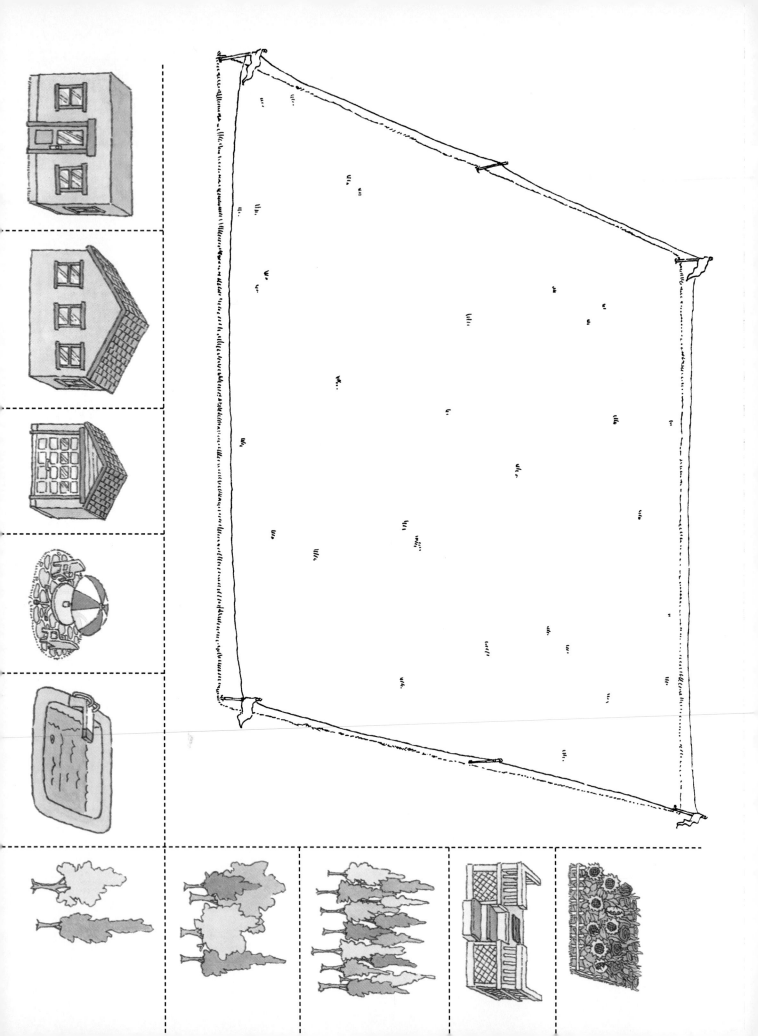